ON ROMULUS, WHILE ABEL SLEEPS
[*A CHTHONIC SONG.*]

On Romulus, While Abel Sleeps [*A Chthonic Song.*]
© 2019 Justin Limoli

Published by Plays Inverse Press
Pittsburgh, PA
www.playsinverse.com

ISBN 13: 978-0-9997247-5-0

First Printing: June 2019
Cover art and design by David Watt
Page design by Tyler Crumrine
Printed in the U.S.A.

**PLAYS
INVERSE**

ON ROMULUS, WHILE ABEL SLEEPS
[*A CHTHONIC SONG.*]
JUSTIN LIMOLI

PLAYS INVERSE PRESS
PITTSBURGH, PA

2019

Dedication Scene

To Kuma,

Let these words act as the scene where all
my characters lay down their
arms/lines/flowers
in remembrance of you
before, the infinite during
and the briefest after.

Prologue [Curtain Rises to *Sun* and *Moon.*]

[*The Sun* wilts, and the curtain rises, revealing a clock ticking the remaining words away. 12:00 strikes, chiming bells and whistles quietly, and *Song* steps forward confronting the murmuring glow of *The Audience* as they return from a long spell of sleep. *Song* finds an ambered instrument breathing for the first time, and takes a sip from it. *Song* drinks into a deeper depth from the instrument, finds its pitch, painting a melody long past remembered, stale in forgotten. *Painted Melody* willows ivy over arpeggio. *Song* continues deep into measure, until a crescent split opens from *Song's* forehead. *The Finale* reaches out of the contracting crescent split, wriggling free from birth. *Silence* dances with *Quiet*, as *The Finale* stands, bows, breathes, for a moment stopping the narrative music. *The Finale* takes the open *Song* and finds where the mouth goes, what strings to pluck, and what pedals sustain or dampen the color. The wilted *Sun* sinks to absence, mute-melodic and lightless, as *The Finale* plays *Song's* ending. *All* is quiet and speechless; the landscape, a whispered spindle weaving the inked ocean out. *The Moon* drifts up noteless, tasting light for the first time. Imagine the sound of *The Moon* trying to hold it, as a clock ticks the remaining words away.]

[A character wearing a Grecian mask of poetry steps forward while the shapes in the background shift into sound delicate with motion (the mouth moves, the throat catches, but no words are heard). The character continues to speak, but again, nothing is heard. This continues. The character bows, and exits. Nothing happens for a while, except for the shifting soundscape in the background.]

Words: [After the character departs, *Words*, unheard, takes shape with season, springs from sound.] Hello everyone. Thank you all for coming. I have so much to say, but don't really know how to begin. What you are about to see, I can only imagine. I'm nervous, truly. I have never been, nor will be, an accomplished performer. But that isn't the point. I want to share with you something truly important. You see [Singing through a muted mouth.], you are about to witness a play that calls itself a play, acts like poetry, with unprepared lines read by an unprepared cast. But remember that this play is about forgiveness led by a character who cannot forgive. [Bows, and disappears in solstice.]

A Beginning After

[The night is lit in its own dreamscape, dreaming its stars away. I don't know if the night dreams, or if that's the point. A character steps forward onto the stage. The stage blinks, and sprouts an orchid nursery. The character is introduced by the rhythmic silence as *Romulus*. His shoulders are hunched and wordless in a draped posture. *Romulus* walks into the sprouted nursery, where he is met by his screaming array of plants and discarded instruments. He tries to welcome them, but instead, his lips shape a tuneless painting, jittery and out of focus. He goes over to a sun hanging loosely by strands of static, turns the bells and whistles, water dancing over-abundant in his watering can.]

Romulus: [Finding his voice among the screaming plants.] Everyone is screaming. Why?

[*The Sun* begins to sing in a brassy tenor to a listening array of plants. *Romulus* hums along, while bobbing the watering can, feeding his plants' hungry mouths. His plants surround him: growing, dying, blooming, screaming. Red, with its roots tangled and tapped into the nutrient vein of blue, blue twisting around the tinged lips of orchids, roses before, roses after, and jasmine is scented with the wrong color. The air surrounds, breathing heavy on the petals. *The Sun* begins to sway to its commanding lyric, voiced and resonant. *The Plants* are singing as a floral choir. Some bloom wings, carried off by a harmonic breeze. *Romulus*, overwhelmed by image, grabs onto something staccatoed and eye-iris scented.]

The Plants: No, we're not screaming, just you.

Romulus: Everyone is screaming.

Everyone: No, just you. You are screaming.

Romulus: Maybe I'm just dreaming in a screaming way.

The Plants: What are you dreaming?

Romulus: My brother. There is so much that is wrong with that image. I'd like to think that he is growing. But even in dreams, he never is. He isn't the bloom or the bud; the word bled into the lyric.

Everyone: I'm not quite sure what that means, but it sounds beautiful, yet you were screaming.

Romulus: [Breathe. Again.] No, I need quiet.

                                                    Enter *Voice from Above.*

Voice: [Takes a sip of all the scents singing.] What are you trying to say?

Romulus: What am I trying to say? [A contemplative *Pause* is watered to thirst.] Who knows? I'm tired of greetings. Leave me alone, all of you.

[His surroundings begin to shrivel. The soil becomes salted sunlight. *The Sun* pales glossed to curtained *Moon*, no longer singing. The scene is splitting from the seams.]

My brother, he is

now what

I am trying to say,

really, my brother,

constant, another present

somewhere within

my plants singing

my words losing what

they mean to say, their

intentions carried off,

mine again, brother how

we say 'different'

with the same syllabic

count, begin our stage again,

losing this breath

differently, these flowers

echoing the dirt,

the texture, the coloring scales,

each sequence from here on, afterwards

remember that I slept

differently when you were

not so close, looking back,

here I am,

in my plants, pretending

the same narrative as the last,

except here, I need to tell you that,

just that, no, I need

to write you down,

losing my breath, never read,

we are different, and I don't know if this ends

with us ending in sequence, in arms,

wordlessly held together, remember

when it was safe to hold you, as an

impossible sharp, these written pages, delicately

unbreakable, the slightest phrase tongued

to language, written and ruined

in character to tell you

how I—

[*Rose*, smoking on a cigarette, interrupts with a thorn.]

Rose: Apologies, but you were sleeping again.

[*Romulus* wakes in his nursery. There are crystalline cloud formations circling inside to a gray pour. The roof is can-opened by an imagined wind. The plants stare back at *Romulus*, not so much a look of worry, but expectation.]

Romulus: I'm not very good at it, apparently.

[It begins to rain inside. *Romulus* walks over to his onyx armor-plated writing desk hidden away in a mist-canopy of roses. There is an old book, drowsy and snoring gently.]

Rose: [Sees the book and grabs it. The book is titled *Bloodletting in Minor Scales*. *Rose* fondles through the pages.] Who wrote this?

[*Rose* looks at the cover, sees the author's name, and looks at *Romulus*. *Rose* reads out some passages.]

Romulus: [Remembering that this isn't supposed to happen.] I did. I wrote it full of blame and hope. [He hides in a page of his own doing.]

[*Rose* continues to read aloud.]

Rose: You're interrupting! [Fondles further pages.] Jesus! You have Heart as a character? Wait until I tell him! He'll love this.

[*Romulus* reaches out and plucks a petal. *Rose* dies, shriveling back to life inside *Pantry, the Oracle of the Past*, serenely statued in pose next to his desk. Suddenly, there is a howling flash of singed orange blossom, and *Pantry* is caught in a trance: a vision of the past. It begins with *Pantry's* tongue twisting unpronounced in an atonal language (Help! Help! Canned corn on the cob! Pickled fish scales! Fermented prune juice! Lactose-infused caviar!). The trance then coils around the body, the past constricting the contortionist. *Pantry* in its night-brass breastplate and petal-silk veil, shifts from oval to octagonal, touched bare and wedded under the weight of memory's anachronistic gaze.]

Rose: [Frantically knocks inside *Pantry* seizing in recollection.] Let me out! Let me out! I didn't even get to the good part! [Instructed by something canned and expired to burn a saged hearing horn as penitence.]

Voice: [Sings.] Let him out.

[*Romulus* closes his eyes, and reverts everything back from memory. *Pantry* smiles, free to statue again in the present.]

Rose: [Dusts off the pollen.] Jeez, I was just kidding. [Mumbles something.] I actually thought some of it was pretty good.

Romulus: [Rolls up the torn petal, smokes, breathes, remembering
             from memory a melody he left under the lines now molding
             behind a door. Sings.] *Was there a purpose in your mother's*
             suffering? Was there a purpose in your mother's suffering? Was there
             a purpose in your mother's suffering?

                                              Enter *Chorus.*

             I don't know, but she broke me into [Transmigrates (octaves are
             lowered and raised simultaneously).] decimals. [His eyes reflect
             the depth of a lost, red ocean, reflecting on the words.]

Voice: That part was beautiful.

Romulus: [Eyes revert back to still-life movement.] What was the fucking
             point though? [He closes his eyes. *In memoria*, he is back
             in that room, left in the conclusion of the last play, holding
             the conductor's baton, the finale singing away the perfect
             conclusion. Except the room was a stage, and he was out of
             breath.] This [Grabs the conductor's baton from the opening
             pages of *Bloodletting*.] looks so stupid now. [The baton blooms
             a rabbit to prove it. The rabbit wilts.]

Rose: [Looks up towards *Voice*.] I think it's time for us to leave. I
             don't like it when he gets like this, all [Searches.] abstract.

     [*Rose* grays to blue petals with each step, leaving.]

Romulus: Wait! No, please, [The room, as a room, lost remembered.]
             stop! I—

Rose: [Gone.]

     [*Romulus* looks up to *Voice*.]

Voice: [Gone.]

     [*Romulus* looks for *Pantry* in the jasmine fields.]

Pantry: [Gone.]

[*Romulus* goes back to his writing desk and begins scribbling until he hears the conductor's baton suddenly tapping against *Timpani*. A phantomed *Remus* appears holding the conductor's baton, wearing a moonless night, shifting the wraith-whispered music to a strange tempo.]

Remus: [Tap, tap, and tap.] Shall we get started?

Romulus: [Closes his eyes.] No, I'm not ready.

[The orchestra plays a sleepless dream, as *Romulus* is unwritten, eye tick-twitching, wordless. *No, I'm not ready.*]

Character List

[There is a chair scripting the character list, leg pointing at certain parts of the narrative, coughing again nacre. The room is unrecognizable. The door is red, a closed opening. There is a sound of a sad ocean in the corner forming swells, the chair dry sinking, and underneath, origami birds screeching. Inside, fingers belonging to this room tap, a figure enters without *Chair 1* noticing, enters the character list, the quiet drowning, the sad ocean in the corner now flooding, the setting upended and unrecognizable. *Chair 1* turns as the figure approaches. A voice from above isn't heard. The swelling tides to red. The waves quell. The door is red, opening shut, breaking the surface, flooding over. Inside this room, there is an unrecognizable setting where *Romulus* sits on a chair attempting to draft a character list.]

Romulus: *Che ci faccio qui?* {What am I doing here?} [Drops what he was writing and continues to think on top of a stooped *Chair 1*.]

Chair 1: [Picks up the crumpled paper, and reads aloud, quietly.] Character List: Character List is now bearded, wine-bottled, and wearing a sailor's outfit. He has aged salted and oceaned over. He finds himself alone, floating on his back in the middle of a sunken ocean at night. The wine bottle is lanterned, illuminating flat waves, fogged calls for help from a setting sun, and the directions he isn't floating towards. With his other empty hand, he begins pouring libations on the northern stars. A salty chill rises, ingesting everything in it. He begins to drift beyond the borders of comprehension, beyond and above the northern stars floating by. The wine bottle tips, pours out the red pigment of a new moon. The after-red liquid solidifies under the pull of tide, reaches for clouds, and becomes a hungry little sky. For a moment, his thoughts are carried off by fish glowing beneath how The Moon glows, reflecting a dripping surface. *I'm lost as a reflection.*

Romulus: [Translate to mother-tongue: I'm lost as a reflection.] *Mi sono perso come un riflesso.*

Chair 1: [*Chair 1's* voice grows buoyant in high tide.] All is quiet as a reflection in a turbulent ocean. Character List is drifting, trying to understand where the surface breaks. Finding it, his grip tightens in crisis, trying to draw closer to the water. His breath takes in blue as a result, sinking further. With so much attention tied to the body as flotation, the stars, left to their own devices, happily dangle in dissent from Character List's compass. How the wine is red, the ocean filled by memory, and the stars shining alongside a blue salted sun, account for Character List losing his bearings.

Romulus: *Dove stai andando?* {Where are you going?}

Chair 1: [Continues, while following *Character List* to the bottom of a lost undercurrent.] Character List reaches the bottom and breathes in. He breathes, hearing chanting from all the ocean's ghosts in confusion: *Ricorda, c'è stato uno scopo nella sofferenza di tua madre? Ricorda! Ricorda!* Character List breathes, completely submerged, suffocating on memory. For a moment, everything is wrong, deafening, remembered. He closes his eyes, waiting for the drowning to pass.

Romulus: [The room becomes flooded with fire and pearls. *Ricorda,* meaning, remember. Memory growing to ocean. No, I don't want to, hearing the slash of blue across the wrist; eyes turn to water, water to red blooming. The melodic image of the room as water fire cools back to padded walls again. *Ricorda.* After coughing up water and feathers.] *Cosa succede dopo?* {What happens next?}

Chair 1: [Growing older in its voice.] Character List opens his eyes, soggy from deafened sight. Atlas comes into focus, pulls him in, breathes a living hymn into Character List's mouth. A siren approaches, playing the wine bottle in orange-clove octaves, the wind stringed and wound to the glass body. The stars inside the compass begin to glow with percussive syncopation. The siren wears garments of struck glass, and the scent of a shipwrecked sea. The siren moves to lyric, singing the bodies of our lost songs to sleep. A red moon descends to dance. Character List and Atlas gaze into one another, not speaking the sound, the depth of it risen.

Romulus: [Eyes dark-rimmed now, the hours expired, a lack of sleep knowing what always happens next.] What happens next?

Chair 1:   I don't know. [The crumpled paper burns wet away. In its place, a single salt-flower in bud. *Chair 1* goes to pot it in sand and drift.] I liked that ending.

Romulus: No, something terrible always happens. [Takes the crumpled paper and begins to read from the ending.] The red ocean rises, forms as a voice of memory, my mother, she... [No, it would be so easy and clean to just end it there. *Ricorda. Ricorda. Ricorda.*] The scene unseams into a broken image, all to black. Character List wakes and finds himself still surrounded by the ocean's ghosts vacant-eyed and silent-chanting. The scene ends under the drowned waves of a crumpled piece of paper. [The salt-flower shatters.]

[The red door of the unrecognizable setting opens. A pair of hands gently lead *Romulus* away to another room, padded and sealed away. A man is sleeping, while scribbling on a notepad.]

Enter *Freud.*

[*Chair 2* is also introduced, sleeping and taking notes diligently. *Chair 1* is thrown in quietly as to not wake the two sleeping characters. *Chair 1* makes a mental note calling for help.]

Freud: [Awakened by the loud scribbling of *Chair 1's* prosaic mental note.] Well, thank God courtesy is dead! Please take a seat.

Romulus: [Confused, but obedient.] Yes, I think sitting would be a good idea.

Freud: [Annoyed.] I was talking to the chair.

[*Chair 1* sits. *Romulus* sits on *Chair 1. Chair 1* creaks in silence.]

Romulus: [To *Freud* and *Chair 2.*] What were you both writing?

Freud: [One eye droops back to sleep.] I was interpreting my dreams. It's much easier than people think [Checks his notes.] Ah! And thanks to you and that anxious-looking rocking chair friend of yours, I didn't even get to the steamy stuff!

Chair 2: And let me introduce myself to you wetdream-interrupti, as well. My name is Dr. Chair 2 and I'm finishing up on my latest book, "Making Nonsensical Sense of Stream-of-Unconsciousness." [Pauses for a reaction. Blank looks, and a nervous cough.] It's a working title. [Extends a leg for them to shake. They do so.]

Freud: [Checks his schedule.] You are a couple centuries early, or late [Shrugs, after conferring with a frail moon-dial.], the point being, you are not on time, and have ruined a perfectly good [Crosses his legs. Coughs.] scientific, [Forgets to wipe the drool.] unconscious metaphor I was having. [Again, blank looks and a nervous cough.] Well, let's get started since you are [Pokes *Romulus* to make sure.] definitively—

Chair 2: And irrationally!

Freud: Yes, and irrationally here. [Straightens an imagined bow tie.] So you unpunctual depressive, tell me about your mother.

[*Romulus* is quiet.]

Did she suffer?

[*Romulus* is quiet.]

I see. So if I apply that to my patent-pending formula on neuroses, if you have a mother, and she suffered, I should then ask you... [The frail moon-dial transforms into an emotional *Abacus*. *Freud* calculates, miscalculates, inadvertently divides the setting by 0 at one point (flooding, fire, and pearls briefly), sets the number to its absolute value, draws a lewd graph illustrating Point A to Point B, applies it to an anti-hieroglyphic language.] Eureka! Was there a purpose to your mother's suffering? [*Abacus* faints back to a Victorian moon-dial.]

Romulus: [Thinking to have been composed, begins to shake. The room floods with a drowning light. No one can breathe. A crackling sound approaches from above. The red door turns into an ocean of closed doors, almost laughing.] No, please, I'm not ready.

Freud: [Draws from his pipe and checks the time through the thinly veiled, unconscious lace of the moon-dial.] I see. Well, you did get here prematurely. This is supposed to happen much later.

[*Freud* closes his eyes, and resumes his work. A pair of hands lead *Romulus* away.]

Exit *Romulus.*

[*Romulus*, Inside a Room, a Silent Memory Skipping.]

Romulus: [Sitting in a contracted position on the floor, remembering. The room shifts with colors swooning darker, a faint glow breaks, acting as the horizon.]

[A phonograph skips, and his fingers percussive-tick on the walls. He is alone now with a memory.]
…the tub, the swollen water, lukewarm,
the tub, the swollen water, lukewarm, the taste,
my lips, the air I kept inside, Dear brother, the blood fauceting out, my length pinned down as I look up at you, so much of me unmoved on the ground, my nose blunted, touch where my lip splits (please don't), the drops of the familiar taste of copper bile-tongued down my throat, Dear brother, the unpleasant bitten warmth of it as I couldn't breathe, the tub, the swollen water, lukewarm, my face showed something forgotten reflected, a feeling expressed of not wanting you home, we were drinking as we do, Dear brother, earlier how you told me you loved me, naked and a beaten image in front of a mirror later, my face contorted into a face I do not recognize as my own, I want to let go as my skin holds it pieced together, I slept next to dad that night as mom tended to you, and what I have for you now I cannot express with the words I have…

[There is a scene where a mother tries to kill herself, but comes home later. Her son/ who called her a cunt/ who called her a cunt/ a cunt/ cuckoo!/ a cunt/ cuckoo!/ cock-a-doodle-do! returns from prison, and she gets woken up by the eldest son crowing now an unhinged call, whose nose is broken, *Blood* crawls to its feet, and *Blood* being *Blood*, well, bleeds, tapping impatiently on the bed stand. Wake up! Wake up!]

The song catches on the phonograph

Dear brother, my face pigmented delicately by your fist
humming through a painful melody of the cloud
depicting an unshaped rain, your fist teaching
me to stay still, your fist crafting the delicate
illusions of the most brittle parts we have left, the swollen
water, lukewarm, my eyes looking up at yours, as your fist

would answer, searching for the right
words, brother, please let me go, as you had this
look followed by you wanting me like this
for so long, such a long echo, warmth and red
pooling out from my mouth, my nose, down my throat,
your fist the most intimate sound, your fist
red with me, red with red, your fist was all
the time it took away, your fist was telling me how
you've changed, now that you were home
from prison, again, home from prison
again, home not home, how you've done this
before to others, and you could hurt absolutely
anyone, a fist so far reaching, keeping my place
on the floor, your fist telling me you would not be coming
back, your fist was choking on all the things it needed
to say, I guess we have never been very good
at expressing ourselves without violence,
your fist was a clenched hand that wouldn't be
held, your fist belonging to you, the unit
to measure the distance between us, calling on the delicate
flame it held, the crushed petals, your first time
fragrant with touch, reciting the lost repetitions of a dead
language, your fist muting my wording of loving
you, your fist saying 'this is how brothers die,' in arms
we die, your fist choking the night air breathless, the sounding
moon waning flickers, illuminating my red on your knuckles,
your fist growing and growing, starting in the womb,
the sounds it was making against my cheeks
rhyming with repetition, remembering
how we would hold them when younger,
your fist tracing the curvature of my face, the rest
of the body limp and numb and flush, unsatisfied,
your fist shaping me in its image, an unlocked portrait
of a sad clutch of red drawing back, again and again,
your fist as the current of all the wilted flowers in bud, the
salted heat eclipsing itself with a red mist, my body as a stain,
the floor as the tapestry, your fist reacting to failing
words, falling, just listen, try to hear the raw need
in what I'm trying to say, all of this ending
in a continual whimper, your fist because

I told you how I blamed you for so much,
your fist blooming into a prismed silence, a spectral call
for quiet, cheering from the chorus as your fist anoints
liquid mercury to my lips, the sign to all that I have
succumbed to your weight, wordless.

Brother, if you called for purple, I would give you amethyst
from my mouth; if blue, water and a sail.

The Blank Page Scene; or, "A Quiet Page Is Left as a Gathering Place"

How *Abel* Sleeps after the Yelling Has Stopped

[*Rose* sits in the heavy touch of a buried room offstage. In the center of the room, there is an unhinged moontower hunched and reaching as a *faux beacon* with unquiet light. After *Rose* finishes *Bloodletting* (remember '*this is the last line that plucks away at my mother's body*'), *Moontower* repeats the final line that plucks away at her body, shadows briefly, and returns with a copy of this play. *Rose* takes it and begins to read out loud to all within the room. *Moontower* dims to an eclipse. The room wanes to darkness, filled with *Rose* calling the current scenes of this play to action.]

Rose: [After turning to a blank page scene, looks up to see *Abel*, seemingly awestruck.] So what do you think so far?

Abel: [Too close.] I don't know! Honestly, I haven't been paying too much attention.

Rose: [Shrugs.] I see. Well, at least you're being honest.

Abel: Yep, and honesty killed me.

Rose: [Rolls his eyes, not taking the bait, instead opting to continue reading. *Abel* stares at *Rose* with a twitching smirk, waiting for the cue to elaborate. A fly lands on *Abel's* eye, applying its digestive fluids, rubbing its feeders greedily, lapping up the iris. *Abel* doesn't blink. The smirk continues to twitch. Suddenly, *Rose* is poked by a disfigured and misinterpreted character, who scurries away. *Rose* sighs a blue red in green, and looks up again.] How so?

Abel: [Brightens.] So I have this brother, right? And we've always our differences, the shepherd and the gardener, but overall, we've always been civil towards each other. I was loved most [Sip.], and one night, you see, we were discussing [Sip.] something, I can't remember, but I'm sure it had something to do with his anger issues [Sip.], and jealousy towards me, since [Sip.] I was loved most. We went to a field... [Drifts. A long sip now: Cabernet, rose water, red sea, empty. Continues to drink, lost in it.]

[*Rose* slowly peers back to reading from the previous scenes, not paying

23

attention to *Abel*. The fly continues to feed. *Abel* has not blinked.]

[With a mouth full of current that spills forth, parting to the floor.] He stabs me with a spade! Can you believe it? Me, the great Abel! Where do you think the adjective [Homophone sic.] came from? You go to a nice, quiet field to stargaze and then nonchalantly tell a guy he has anger issues. And what does he do? Kills me with a fucking gardening tool. Talk about case in point, right?

Rose: [Sets the play down, sighs again (red blue into a siren of green), folds an earmark on the page, on the cusp of the part where the two brothers are about to exchange heads.] I thought you both erred over your drinking issues?

[There is a pause.]

Abel: What do you mean? I don't have a drinking problem. [Drinks.]

Rose: According to your file, he brought you to his field because you came home drunk, and he didn't want your mother to see you like that. You then urinated on his newly created Halcyon Remembered Hallelujah Proteas, while ranting about how much better and loved you are than him.

Abel: That's not true. And even if that were to happen, plants are dumb. Herding and animal husbandry are where the *real* money is at. God told me that in a dream. Let it be known. [Sip.]

Rose: I see. Well, do you remember how you died?

Abel: Oh, do I! I was showing him the constellation God made me for my latest and greatest sacrifice (the first of my little firstlings), when he suddenly went ballistic and—

Rose: No. You jumped on top of him after he blamed you for your parents' unhappiness. You then started beating him (your fists/ singing their need for red/ their thirst for love/ let it be known/ as our quiet song). He was able to reach for a spade you

24

knocked over, and [Slides a finger along the throat.] now you're here.

[*Abel* closes his eyes and continues to drink. *Rose* goes back to reading. After a while, the bottle tips over, replenished with empty. *Abel* curls, eyes heavy, into a small and slender sleep. The fly brassy monotone buzzes to the song 'Things don't really change around here' playing on a tuneless old clock hiding a piano. In a secluded corner, *Cain* slouches and sways back and forth.]

Cain: ...And then she asks, "Cain,
                   where is your brother?"
                   [hear his cries from the soil] For I am his
                   keeper. Yes, for I am
                   his keeper. What have I
                   done? What have I done? [hear his
                   cries] And then she asks,
                   "Cain, where is your brother?"
                   [from the soil] For I am his keeper. Yes,
                   for I am his keeper. What have I done? [hear
                   his soiled cries from] What have I done? And then
                   she asks, and then she asks, and then she
                   asks, "Cain? Cain! Cain?!
                   where is your
                   brother?" [the soil, the soil, his cries
                   from the soil] [hear it, hear it] For I am his
                   keeper. Yes,
                   for I am his keeper.
                   I am his
                   keeper, his keeper; for I am
                   Cain
                   What have I done?

[Continues, cursed to never stop. An imaginary dull spade self-inflicts to puncture, while *Abel* sleeps.]

[A Hidden *Song* Plays.]

[Inside the hidden piano *Romulus* is found digging, descending, striking the ground with liquid strokes, how he paints the earth deeper, uprooting harmony underground, where he finds the afterlife, digging past it, uprooting how he moves, his name is *Romulus*, the one who digs deeply, finding the common source, ore let's keep this, quiet please, how he digs, finding water underneath water, mixed with dirt, mixed with his dirt, he drinks it, digging further, not the sound he intends, his wrists are broken, knees locked in march, there is snow underground eating away at how his wrists break, using the clanging sound of his fingers, he eats the dirt in his fists, how he thinks of it as his own, seeing his movement tied down, how he digs with his hands, on his knees locked, north becomes north below the dirt, a monument underground, unearthed the statue, a plant growing beneath, blooming mud sceneries, how the scent gets left growing, the monument to the monument, becoming a road, digging as a road with pedestrian crossings, how new the scenery is, taking pictures and then back to digging, the smiling, the dirt forming another layer of separation, digging, at the level where stars are shining, not shining, dull like dirt, looking up and seeing the ground, digging how he digs without asking for recollection, collecting all the broken bones in the ground, now there is a sky below, building foundations caused by severe lack of memory, rattling how the earth quakes, forgetting how things are supposed to shake if buried deep enough, the strongest resistance to moving down, how we shape with mud, let it harden later, but for now dig, dig like this, dig like someone has strapped you down with their body, and you are convulsing from love for this person, rejecting your own impulse to breathe, and now there is a moon warmer than the one you used to hide behind, dig dig dig, you want them to keep telling you, if only you had fingers in your mouth choking the moon, now the sun, how the fingers want you to dig, how happy your mother is going to be, and there are keys buried next to locks that don't fit the way they should underground, how far down the fingers go, and his fingers are scratching the neck, infected with dirt, how it will rot over is a question buried next to the one great sentence that creates an eclipse imagery of sun and moon, now there is Hell laden with springs and fountains, a mountain perched on a dark figure's shoulder, how it is frozen, says it loves you more than you as a dark sentence eclipsing, and there is a claret playing a cornet here, which you will name, forget the name, forget the face belonging to the name, forget, just continue breathing in, tasting like dirt, the fingers wet with you, wrapping around your neck, calling you what your neck never did, affectionately you will forget how you were strangled, pinned down, pining, your nose bleeding, how he snorted more than just your smell, (*Cocaine* sings a song about addiction, forgets some of the words, and *The Audience* applauds politely.) how you are bigger than him, but it doesn't matter because he is showing you something, something that you want to bury, how to point this out on a map for later, how you are older than him and should know that your nose is probably broken, that you have orchids that need watering, how you want to learn to play this song with blooms, turn this into a tragedy in the morning after coffee, ask yourself where are you trying to bury, why are you here, how is he so angry, looking down at you with red, trapped in a look of hate and love, the only colors you remember, how to tell you that he has an addiction to red, how you see it in the way he speaks, an impediment of red, his hair gray with red, looking older than he should, his color already a muddy red digging, how he shakes, how he looked sorry the next morning, how he said he didn't mean to, wasn't ready to hear the things he asked you to reveal, how I wasn't ready to hear him say—]

Remus: Do you know mom tried to kill herself?

[*Romulus* descends a little further and finds a buried *Stage*.]

[A Pair of Hands Pull *Romulus* into *Mental Ward*.]

Romulus: What am I doing here, mentally?

Ward: Well, you put yourself here, to put things simply.

Romulus: I don't understand. I was underground.

Ward: Look at your surroundings, and tell me where you are.

Romulus: [Looks around.] I'm not sure, but I feel quietly safe though.

Ward: Why?

Romulus: Too much has happened. I was losing control over everything. I
                was in a hole digging, overwhelmed with language, waxing
                silently poetic.

Ward: Look at your surroundings, and tell me why that is.

       [*Romulus* looks at his surroundings. He lets his hands streak against the
       walls. The quiet in the room hangs naked by a red silk veil.]

       [Continues.] You've been drinking.

Romulus: [Takes another sip from the horn of plenty. It fountains
                over, waterfall spilling. *Romulus* chokes, hands shaking.] And
                writing. More importantly, writing.

Ward: So, what have you been writing?

       [Another sip. *Do you know mom tried to kill herself?* Pause. *Romulus*
       imagines himself underground with the birds, the clouds, the bones of
       our gardens.]

              [*Ward* starts slitting down the middle, pooling into an
              opening.] Never mind. It will start how it is supposed to and in
              due time.

       [*Romulus* is led by *Voice* to a locked room. *Voice* misleads him inside.
       Romulus begins nervously in a room, planting his things, orchids in a
       strange sense shifting into orchids locked in a room, how *Abel* is

sleeping, the sound of *Remus* threatens, threatening to kill himself, just like how their mother shares the same ending and epilogue, both threatening how many times to end, except everything stems from how *Remus* calls for help in a strange sense, shifting into orchids locked in a room, how *Romulus* watches, being asked to speak, how he can't speak, how he doesn't want to, how he tries to get away from his orchids shifting into his mother blaming him for not speaking, how he can't speak without interfering with the narrative, how *Remus* calls for help and *Romulus* doesn't speak.]

Romulus: [Watering.] My orchids are dying.

Voice: [Watching the orchids shift into an oblique light.] So your mother tried to kill herself?

Romulus: [Overwatering.] I wrote a book about it, and it took me almost until the second act to admit this.

Voice: Is she okay?

Romulus: [No more light locked away in a room.] No.

[*Room* writes this down.]

No, she isn't okay. She isn't doing well. I don't know what I did to imply closure. I can't escape well enough to gain closure. I want out of this. I need to get away. But I'm here, caught in the same fucking narrative, and I can't write towards anything, escape towards anything. [Honestly.] Things weren't meant to turn out like this.

[*Voice* approaches.]

Voice: Am I helping?

Romulus: [The orchids are choking.] I'm tired of growing. I'm tired of thinking about what you might say to me, and what I will consequently say to you, your intentions of growth. I just want to stay here in this room, forgiving, tending to my orchids. [The pour becomes empty.]

Voice: [Aromatic rose light reveals *Voice* belongs to *Romulus*.] Now everyone is willing to say things like "I may just kill myself." And you listen to it. And you think to yourself, "They used to keep it to themselves."

Room: [As an encompassing swarm of sounds screaming.] Now everyone is willing to say things like, "I may just kill myself."

Romulus: Now everyone is willing, so they say, "I may just," killing themselves.

                                                        Enter *Ward*.

Ward: I think it's time you look at yourself.

[*Ward* plucks *Orchid's* head from the stem, snaps his fingers, the stem dies into *Mirror*, the thoughts leaving, drifting down towards *Voice* above the room. *Orchid* becomes *Reflection*. *Romulus* sees *Reflection*, *Reflection* sees *Justin* instead. *Reflection* wipes away the rest of the blurry image of *Romulus*. *Justin* relents. The room is now filled with *Justin*, the broken mask of *Romulus* seeing what it's been hiding.]

Justin: So here I am again, interpreted as feeling sorry for myself.

[*Ward* picks up the discarded mask of *Romulus*, and dons it. *Ward* becomes *Cliché*.]

Cliché: I think you are placed in a particularly bad situation. That's what I think, anyway.

Justin: [Honestly.] I was hoping it wasn't going to turn out like this again.

Cliché: So what are you going to do?

Justin: Admit that I carry so much blame for others and it has brought me here in this room, locked away, talking to characters that don't exist, realizing that I exist as so many characters.

[*Justin* slits *Mirror*, resulting in *Cliché* growing into a pair of hands that take *Justin* back to *Stage*. *Justin* snaps his fingers and the discarded shovel left in the previous scene becomes *Shovel*.]

Shovel: [Cuts through the dirt of *Everything*.] Oh no/ hello!

[*Justin* bends down and begins tickling *Stage*.]

Is that really necessary?

Justin: I'm about to do terrible things to show you how I feel. It would be nice to hear something pleasant before that happens.

[*Stage* erupts in the sound of something spoiled spoiling over again. *The Audience* spills out from *Periphery*. They take their seats again, muttering sharp consonants without vowels. *Shovel* attempts to leave, but cannot. *Shovel* relents and takes a seat. *Justin*, alone on *Stage*, bows.]

Thank you all for coming. Nothing has changed.

[*Stage* erupts in applause.]

[*The Can* Singing to His Miscued Opening.]

The Can: Hello, and good morning [Correction.] evening, ladies and gentlemen of the jury. What a gorgeous whatever we're having. Such lovely everything. You are all gathered here to pass judgment; me, this plot, hello it's me again, the ending, the narrator, yourselves. Hello, ladies and gentlemen of the jury. [*The Can* darkens, sharp.] Hello. May I present to you [Sing., correction, pl.] something truly sequential: the sequel!

[*The Can* reveals it, the body marked with needles, corroded arteries, pointed objects injecting their saliva, such spit flying like little notes of tapestry. *The Sequel* muttering for more, just enough, no, not enough, coughing, shuddering at itself like some great idiot tasting the heaviness in its need to end.]

Justin: [Stretching, still dripping from stitching out of *Romulus*.] He's gone. I don't really care. Do you believe me?

The Can: Why yes! Absolutely not! Ladies and gentlemen of the jury, good evening!

Justin: [Breathing from his chest, slowly upwards, crawling out through his nasal passage. Exit. Breathe more slowly. The hollow weight of it.] My brother is sick.

The Can: Goodness, and hello! Oh no!

Justin: I'm fine, really. The whole thing has just been really peculiar. Bizarre? Just strange. Do you believe me?

The Can: [Whimsically chirping, like two chicks dying, the two my mom brought home. One died, and then the other, the morning after each other. They cried for something for so long, sleep, and wake up to quiet.] I don't know! In fact, I don't really know what I'm doing here. But be warned; you'll regret it!

Justin: [Narrates my regrets.] The Can declares a warning while spitting out generic Tomato Bisque for affect, the soupy character bowing, liquid limbs spilling, enzyme eaten, The Can's rich yellow saliva salivating and tongue hungry on his black and white pinstripes, naked in an old mob suit, slurping on a firing Tommy gun for a spoon, drags the soupy concoction of a bisque character offstage for one-act of violence, how the top flaps open, locked, the memory meaning, Goodness me! the shift to my memory, look at me now, [Shifts.] over here, remember cell bars, the solitary confinement, how this is the third time he is back there, my brother, the prison literacy project, the black eye, the busted lip as speech impeding, the visitation hours, check your pockets, check your pockets, beep! BEEP! check your pockets, the slurred dialect after, how he was homeless because we couldn't, how he couldn't, after a while you remember, I'm pretty sure he is gone, each time thinking the same thing, for good this time, yes, *For good this time.*

[An unnoticed *Clock* strikes that time before or after it happens, *Chorus* as *Cuckoo* flapping out on the incorrect hour, petal rose feathers flying to the singed scent of time.]

Cuckoo: [Squawk chime.] For good this time! For good this time! For good this time!

[*The Minute* passes with its little steps of seconds. *The Clock* swallows up *Chorus* until the next untuned hour resumes. Silence.]

The Can: [Miscues his return to scene, wiping his mouth.] That's right! [Menacingly.] This is the part where I—

[*The Can*, now completely stripped and formed in a naked, calloused reach, gestures to the unnoticed *Clock* with a sharp and violent touch. The minutes, seconds, hours, and moon cycles collide and clash, piling noise, to create a deafening cymbal rush.]

It's not nearly loud enough! I can still hear myself think!

[The sharp touch becomes even sharper and draws closer to *Clock's* face; it's little arms and legs begin to tick in past. *Clock* conducts the derailing of concussed time measurements to fortissimo, colliding to crescendo, more and more (tic/toc/tic/tic/10!/9!/8!/tic/toc-toc) frantic and frenetic. *Clock* faints, losing all control over an irregular pulse of time. *The Can* seeing *Clock* raisined in gray withdraws his extended talon; its shape for a moment molded to a cleaver.]

[After appreciating his handiwork, takes an unhinged door, shouting over *Time's* ticking drumroll.] Ladies and gentlemen of the jury, I give you— [*The Can* opens the unhinged door to reveal a sleeping *Jason*, my brother. Not other names, like *Julian*, his middle name, the same as my father's, or *Remus*, after my attempts at an accurate *Romulus*. Ladies and gentlemen of the jury, please try to forget my poor pseudonyms, and forgive them. I'm going to struggle to find words as *Justin*, to tell you about my brother. How I blame him for *Bloodletting*, how I didn't really say that before, how anxious my mother gets after she catches his voice, how angry everything is. He is an addict, and I am his brother.] Ta-dah!

[*The Can* slicks back his hair, pirouettes, looking like my father. Narrates, now sure that his smile is drooling.] 'Your brother got thrown in the can again. Your brother got thrown in the can again.' [Another fantastic spin and bow. *Time's* players get violently muted and dragged away, locked back inside a gray, unmoving clock. Once the shuddering stillness settles, *The Can* looks over, remembering that *Justin* is still there.] Did you hear me? Your brother got thrown in the can again!

Justin: [The scene now reverberates with silence.] He's gone. I don't really care. Do you believe me?

[*The Can*, not listening, fingers plugging his ears, continues to sing off-key over the hanging question.]

The Can: Your brother got thrown in the can, again.

(He's gone.)

Your brother got thrown in the can, again.

(He's gone.)

Your brother got thrown in the can, again.

(He's gone.)

Your brother got thrown in the can, again.

(He's gone.)

[*Stage Direction* finally takes the hint, throwing *Jason* into *The Can's* confining womb, slamming the cell door. *The Can* bows, and exits, still singing.]

A Scene Casting All the Forgotten or Disregarded Names and Characters

[*Justin* walks into the chthonic graveyard.]

Romulus:

Julian:

All gone:

Suicide:

So they say:

Cocaine:

Initially:

My little brother takes:

Meth:

Everything:

Empty:

@4:00 am:

Blank:

My expression sleeping:

The guitar I don't play anymore:

Syringe:

I filled it with spit as a joke:

One time:

His heart should've stopped:

First time:

Cent'anni:

May you live:

1,2,3:

One Hundred Years:

Pantoum:

Chair 3:

Here:

All the poets in the body:

Writing to their rooms:

Cliff:

Hanger:

Falling:

Suicide 2:

To my brother:

How he takes:

This &:

That:

Tit Four:

Tat:

Nox: [Meaning the darker shade of *Memory*.]

Cocaine still: [To *The 4:00 am Heroin(e)*.]

Red and Eros:

Schrödinger: [Cat calls.]

Disbelief: [How I know him then.]

Limp-still on the floor:

How I was slow:

To get up:

Wobble—(v.) To stand ignobly:

When I knew him now:

Addiction: [As the *Unhinged Door*.]

Dan:

Drinks:

My Father:

Drinks 2:

Remains:

My Addictions:

i, Nameless: [Masks over.]

Me:

Here I am:

After everything:

A moment:

    [All rise again as *The Curtain* falls.]

An Episode of Violence (Revisited)

[*Justin* buries the graveyard, *The Moon* sets and *The Sun* is sick. *Justin* paints everything that has happened in a strange tongue dangling, looking like a swollen eye drooling, blinking somehow. *The Sun* coughs, so *The Moon* sets again. *Romulus*, climbs out from *The Moon*, six feet under but tall, wet with consciousness, how it is raining, takes a few steps, clouds forming, remember that this is chthonic, so underground, very much beneath cupped hands leaking, and remembering its objects underground, how it blinks, looking at *Justin* from this distance, how *Romulus* takes *Justin*, having him resort to memory, meaning *Justin* is bleeding, and how his mother must have felt seeing him how he sees himself, so *Justin* walks, and he doesn't mention how it was his brother, but his father knows, and his father tells him that he's sorry, and his father knows what violence looks like, and his father calls him things he hasn't heard in a long time, his brother in another room, in a different body, and *Justin* doesn't know what he says to his mother, but *Justin* scratched his neck, *you got him pretty good*, so his mother says, a dead string is plucked to no sound as he touches it to a painful numbness, she takes off what is left of his torn shirt, whatever he was holding onto, little but substantial, lets go.]

this
　　is
　　　insanity

[The boom of light reverberates the words *I think we*

　　　　　　~~hate~~ ~~hate~~ **hate**

　　　　　　each other, while forced to

　　　　　　~~love~~ ~~love~~ *love*

　　　　　　one another.]

[He starts crying. Something numbing sets in. He thinks his face hurts. He couldn't get up. He is now on the shower floor crying, chanting *this is all fucked*, as the blood from his mouth spits. He doesn't hear what his mom is trying to say. He hears her say something she didn't. He starts yelling at her, blood continuing its spitting monologue, words overlapping.]

it's all happening again, it's all happening {again}, it's all happening {again}, it's all {again} happening, it's {again} all happening, {again} it's all happening

[Maybe he resents her for her capacity to love and forgive, which leads to acceptance. But that would mean closure, and that is something that does not exist in a circular narrative.]

[*The Can* picks up this torn memoir. After reading, *The Can*, naked but draped in wings freshly plucked and unfeathered, looks up at a coughing moon cold fevered in the inked light-nigh(gh)t.]

The Can: Ladies and gentlemen of the jury, even The Moon is sick. [*The Can* bends over backwards, and through his torso, peers into his bars. To *Jason*.] I believe you set in motion a very long list of offenses.

Jason: Not guilty, your Honor.

The Can: Sustained! Well played.

Jason: [Takes a syringe full of alphabet soup.] Not guilty.

The Can: [It's raining portraits of *Justin*. *The Can* picks one up, a Pop-Art caricature of *Justin* as a Neo-Sad Clown in a group-therapy session. The piece is called 'Creative Writing Workshop, or a Shrill Cry for Help! (in C# minor)'.] You are nothing like your brother.

Jason: [Takes something soft, open, and warm. Drops it. The sound, as it shatters.] Not guilty, your Honor, but let the record show that I'll also take that as a compliment.

The Can: [Reaches for him, but retracts that statement.] He blames you for your mother's condition.

Jason: [Forms three lines /// (tercet/ torrent/ turpentine). Wipes his nose, the sinus, the septum, now pupiled and dilated. The warmth sound, again as it shatters.] Do you know my mother tried to kill herself?

The Can: [His hands now sharpened again to cleaver, takes *Jason* and sets him on *The Scale of Justice*.] Yes, I think the point has been made. You are here today to state your innocence on the matter.

Jason: [There is a glitch with the portrait-rain, and a copy of *Bloodletting in Minor Scales* falls elegantly and cringed on the stage. *Jason* picks it up and reads a couple pages.] Huh, so he wrote a book about it. [Continues reading.]

The Can: How do you plead?

Jason: Huh? Oh yeah, not guilty, your Honor. I'll be good, I promise. You see, none of this was really my fault. I'm actually not such a bad guy. I served my time already, and now I'm (varicose violet) clean. [*Jason* inspects the syringe to see if there is any left.]

The Can: Well good! I guess it's settled then. You are free to go.

Jason: Really? That's great. [Fills the syringe with more alphabet soup.]

The Can: [Turns into a loud slice. The rain starts pouring scenes of screaming character breaks.] Ladies and gentlemen of the jury, I believe I am about to pass judgment!

[*The Scale* scaling over sounding *Timpani*.]

Jason: [Stupored speech, as a foreign substance constricts inside the body.] Not guilty! [Nods off to sleep, twirling his hair, growing grayer, older than his first steps.]

The Can: [Points at *Jason*.] Bang! Bang!

Jason: [One eye droops open.] Yes?

The Can: [He is sharp, an inch away from something dark.] Was there a purpose in your mother's suffering?

Jason: Do you know my mother tried to kill... not guilty. [The eye droops back to closed.]

The Can: Wonderful! I don't think he knows how far he has fallen!

Justin: [Seeing this all transpire, feeling the strings lose his grip, muttering to himself.] He doesn't know where mom is right now. I want to set my characters on him; the bad ones, the ones I'm afraid of, the ones I carry deep within me, violent and articulate, articulate with violence, because there is no such thing as closure when he's around.

[*The Can* turns, smiling at *Justin*.]

The Can: I have [A syncopated parade of sounds.] an idea!

[A character falls from the balcony {splat!}.]

Jason: [Sleeps through a sobering sounding.]…

Justin: [Draws closer; still to himself, and to all consequently]. I can't bury what mom is now because of you.

[*The Can* draws close to *Justin* and sings out a whisper. *Justin* is cast to sleep next to *Jason*. *Justin* kicks out, exhausted at his words, his attempts at words, whimpers a little bit. But both brothers, strange in their own ways, in this moment of scene, are mutually sleeping. *I want to paint him in all the seconds of my blame, (Light is scented in Hours)*.]

The Can: Yes, but I'm awful, truly I am. Trust me. [*The Can* opens again, this time revealing the entrance to Hell. *Jason* is dropped somewhere deep. *Justin* is carried inside by a cloaked figure and placed in front of a gate that reads, *Woe to those who find these words inside me. The Can* peers inwards to watch this all unfold, as the stage is finally set.]

[*Justin* Enters Hell Through the Garden of Eden.]

Poseidon: Neptune!

Zeus: Jupiter!

Hades: Pluto!

Pantry: Moon?

The Can: [*Screaming* is heard pirouetting inside *The Can*. To all.] Ladies and gentlemen of the jury, not all people are inherently good. We want to believe that there is a common thread to evil. We want to believe that it can be fixed or changed. Eloquently, I'm here to tell you that you are in fact wrong. There is no greater illusion than repentance.

[*A Voice from Above* is heard.]

Voice: To forgive is divine. To forgive is retribution in itself.

The Can: [Bends over backwards and peers into the scene, singing over a breaking fiddle.] To err is human, to forgive is human, and I am divine, and will never die.

Justin: [Awakens in this new setting, confused.] Hello? Where am I?

All: Hell… we think? This isn't generally where Hell begins. We're in a garden. Things aren't so bad here.

Justin: [Remembers being told by a poem:] 'No one is truly evil.'

Zeus: [Seated on top of a stunted, floral mountain, with *Hera* fidgeting on his lap.] I don't see anything wrong with that conclusion.

[*Justin* is silent. No one is evil; truly.]

Zeus: I'm bored. Come forward, and tell me a secret.

[As *Justin* approaches obediently towards the written command, a snap of fingers is heard as an angry gust of voices, and *Bloodletting* flies out from his mouth. *Hermes* swats it with a lyre.]

Hermes: [Holding *Bloodletting* by a broken wing, the scent of flight and lyric leaking out. To *Zeus*.] Shall I banish it or something?

Zeüs: No, let me have it. [Reads *Bloodletting*. *The Garden* is quiet in petal. *Zeus* closes the flightless book when finished. He engulfs it in his hands, breathes haloed breath into it, and the book becomes an origami unfolded swan again. *Bloodletting* clumsily ascends in a strange flight. *Zeus* thunder claps.] I decree that you wrote the same thing over and over again, expecting a different result. That isn't art.

Freud: [Taking a sleepwalking stroll through the garden.] That's commonly identified as insanity! [Exits through the awaiting nightshade mouth of a cobra lily.]

[Elsewhere, *Neptune* swallows the ocean. *Pluto* converts all his wealth into a small key. *Zeus* leaves and falls asleep in the arms of someone bare-winged and mortal, begetting *Dante*.]

Enter *Dante*.

[*Hera* watches, wanting to look away, watches, no, look away, over and over again, the same results, the ocean swallowing *Neptune*, *Neptune* teaching *Pluto* to drown. *Pluto* plunges the small key into the heart of the ocean, the ocean as beast dies, unlocked. *The Garden* drinks it all hungrily. *Hera* watches, over and over *Zeus* asleep in the arms of a discrete kiss.]

Hera: [Speaking to sight.] Over and over and over, altering nothing. Expecting something different. Please let me leave. [She attempts to.]

Dante: [To *Justin*, seeing *Bloodletting* circling above them, extended.] Nothing has changed, has it?

Justin: Why am I here? I don't want to be here.

Dante: I don't really know. I didn't write it like this. Here, drink this;

it'll quiet the nerves. [Hands *Justin* a glass of sound.]

Justin: [Off.] He comes and goes,
             comes and goes,
             taken away,
             look away,
             locked away.

[*Hermes* calms all of Eden with a harp, ringing with taste sweetly.
The beautiful image of the flowers being painted by a cloaked figure
breathing his final note departs. *Zeus* disregards the companion, and
floats into a loving gesture with *Hermes'* harp singing like an intimate
entrance to Hell. *The Garden* weaves its flowers into wreaths of insanity.
Justin, drunk on sound and seeing *Hera* shaking, reaches for her,
wanting something soft spoken. *Dante* drinks and drunkenly watches
Art begetting *Art*, *Art* as its own insanity, *Hera* and *Justin* lonely and
alone together, *Zeus* looking on, smirking as the two are as clueless
as a question. The music of the flowers hears *Hera's* heart learning its
instruments, *Neptune* forgiving a dead memory of *Odysseus*, and *Dante*
accepting that this has all happened before unwritten.]

Dante: [Stumbles over to a tasting *Justin*, dropping his cup.] You need
             to see something. [He calls *The Can* over, drinking from a
             cherub's fountain.]

Justin: [The music stops; the sound of a record scratch.] How are you
             here?!

The Can: [Blinks a deafening whisper, and all of Hell is dark and quiet.]
             Ladies and gentlemen of the jury, I am impotently omnipotent,
             and therefore elsewhere omnipresent! [Spontaneously still-
             trips.]

[*Justin* looks and sees that all characters have taken their starting
positions, with *Hera* shaking next to *Zeus*, back seated on his throne.
Justin attempts to flee, but *The Can* swoops in, and grabs hold of him
with his talons. He tries to calm *Justin* by feeding him something held
in his beak still kicking, still aware that this is an end. After, *Justin* spits
out each brittle conductor's baton, having never tasted *Harp* before, and
after, the taste of her gone.]

Ladies and gentlemen of the jury, let's proceed with judgment.

[*The Can* claps a directorial clap, and *Hermes* begins playing *Blue's* forgotten hymn. *Pluto* takes his cue and places two gold lips across *Dante's* eyes.]

Pluto: [To *Dante*.] You must lead him.

Dante: I refuse. I like it here. I buried the rest of Hell long ago. I'm not going back.

Pluto: You must.

The Can: [Blinks, and something resembling *The Moon* spills screaming sharp over *Dante*.] You must. [With a wordless look, *Dante* shudders at a sickle sound. After collecting himself, and the sharp edge drifts away from gunpoint, *Dante* agrees. *The Can* then looks at *Justin* shaking.] Don't worry, I feel sorry for you, but this is going to be so horrifyingly fun! [Claps a shrill sound.]

[*Justin* leaves a note behind for *Hera*. {Dear Hera, (but for a flickering flight of light) Yours, Justin} *The Can* reads it, crumples it into an origami sound, and tosses it into the cherub's fountain. The note pearls at the bottom, as its own afterlife.]

All leave except *Dante* leading *Justin*.

[*Dante* and *Justin* Reach a Gate that Leads to the First Layer of Hell.]

Justin: [Crosses an X over his chest, and recites.] There are words
                 inside me. There are words inside me. There are words inside
                 me. There are words… [Continues.]

[The tourmaline blue Gate of Eden opens to reveal the rest of Hell
setting to horizon.]

The Can: You are now entering the first layer of Hell; Segue Styx or the
                 Acheron River. I don't remember, but hurry and get lost!

[*Dante* takes a step, and looks back at a still *Justin*.]

Dante: What's wrong?

Justin: Why am I doing this?

[*The Can* suddenly charges them from behind with two candlelit
thumbs taped to his forehead like a makeshift luminary bull, gores them
forward, and closes the gate.]

Dante: [Remembering that this is how most beginnings occur.] It
                 seems like you don't really have a choice. We can either stop
                 here, or proceed with this epic.

[Suddenly *Charon* appears before them.]

Charon: Two tokens please.

[*Dante* hands over the correct currency. A character in the overheard
distance snaps his fingers. A dry heave of smoke clouds over *Charon*,
and he becomes a sinking gondola.]

Justin: [To *Dante*.] Are we supposed to step in? I don't see any water
                 imagery [The gondola sinks further.], but it looks like it's taking
                 it in though.

Dante: I don't know. I don't know. [Clasps his hands in prayer.] Oh
                 Virgil, what do I do?

                                              Enter *Virgil's Ghost*.

Virgil: I don't know, but Dante, I think I'm dead! What do I do?

[*Justin* steps in and the others follow. Again, a distant snap of fingers is heard, and *Water* runs in an attempt to catch up with the scene. *Water* gangly pirouettes overflowing underneath the sinking gondola. After settling into its corrected surrounding, the gondola jolts sideways slowly like a bare-thighed breath pulling away from the drunken grope of undertow. After *Time* passes them, *Justin* becomes restless, seemingly landlocked on this slow-crawling plank. Hoping that the water is truly cursed with correction as the Acheron River, *Justin* jumps off the static, submerged-but-floating gondola and plummets to the bottom. He becomes flooded with memory and climbs up to the surface.]

Justin: This isn't right! The Acheron River is supposed to take away memory.

Enter *The Can*.

[*The Can* slithers over to the wreckage of *Justin* floating. Reveling in *Justin's* look of powerlessness, snaps his fingers, blessing *Justin* in the water's communion.]

The Can: [Catches his breath after seeing *Justin's* confusion, and after, orchestrates.] Now rise.

[*Justin* crawls to an acute standing position like a pale willowing of blue.]

Justin: Why is this happening? I'm not supposed to retain memory, nor stand on water.

The Can: [Flicks his forked tongue twisted around the throat of a newborn spoon.] Well that wouldn't be very much fun, now would it? We changed that ages ago. We felt that memory is the best catalyst for torture. There is a vindictive persistence to it, especially to those that find themselves here. Anyway, keep going ahead, and remember not to step off the river, or else. [The eyes flash something red and sharp. The tongue constricts. The spoon is lost to memory.] Understood? The others will join you at your destination shortly after. And with that, ciao for now! [*The Can* descends back to flight. Meanwhile, *Dante* looks up stargazing this ever-changing nightscape over the drift-green sounds of a seasick *Virgil* lifesong-mourning back and forth.]

[*Justin* continues along the watered down path as instructed, walking forward with the unsure steps of a sunken sleep. He is about to reach his destination, when, with the last step, a pair of hands pull him back into the water. While submerged, *Justin* is introduced to a chorus of drowning *Stars*.]

Stars: [In unison/all'unisono forming dissonant words in the wet-singed cadence of water.]
Welcome!
Goodbye!
You are—
Good riddance!
Look out!
Hello!
Oh dear!
Wonderful!
No more, please!
Give me that!
Why?
Hello?
Leave!
Who?…WHO?!
Welcome!
It's too late for you!
Yoohoo!
Yoohoo!
Yoohoo!
Cuckoo! Cuckoo! Cuckoo!
Bang! Bang!
Stop, please, stop!
Get off! Get off!
Get off?
Get off!
Please?
No!
Yes!

Welcome! Welcome!
Goodbye.
It's time.
The hour strikes midnight!
And to all a goodnight.
Goodnight!
Sweet dreams!
Oh no…oh no…oh—
…hello?
Quiet hangs in the air.
It's time to go…we need to go…
It's time to say goodbye.
Arrivederci, suckers!
Ciao, mi amore…
Good riddance!
Cuckoo! Cuckoo!
[Clap, clap, clap.]
Shut up! Shut up!
Bang! Bang! Bang!
Applause
Welcome, welcome.
Get out, you son-of-a-bitch!
No, stop!
Oh yes!
Here's looking at you.
Oh, it's you.
You're welcome.
Welcome home.
It's time.
It's time?
It's time.
Goodbye.

[*Justin*, blue-faced and asphyxiated, applauds, asking for an encore. The drowned stars bend a soggy bow. A drowsy door is revealed, and *Justin* enters. He plummets down, and as something resembling the ground grows and grows to greet him, *Justin* lands in a trampolined puddle of scented jasmine. He crawls out of the puddle, and waits for *Dante* and *Virgil*, laughing. He looks up seeing *The Moon* with its door still open, shedding its glow, still an adjusting reflection. *Justin* closes his eyes in a silent field of moonlight.]

[*Sun* Opens, *Morning* Fields.]

[The next morning, *Justin* wakes up finding himself in a field of spectrumed light. The door in *The Sun* opens, and a soaked *Dante* and *Virgil* plummet towards *Justin*.]

Justin: [To *Dante* after landing awkwardly.] How did you get here?

Dante: Well, our transport finally had the decency to sink, and there was a door that we passed through. It was easy enough. Why did you jump off?

Justin: I felt like capsizing from the present, if that makes any sense, so I jumped.

Virgil: It doesn't, and that's a bit dramatic, and might I add, gauche even, don't you think?

Justin: Well, I got here first, if that counts for anything.

[Somewhere off in the distance, a booming laugh is shrieking until cadence. Probably *The Can.*]

Anyway, shall we continue?

Dante: Actually, if it's alright with you, Virgil and I would like to get some rest.

[*Virgil*, seeing their present field, leisurely poses on a couch of wheat and grain, and begins writing a surreal pastoral poem. When finished, he reads it to the other two travelers, putting *Dante* in rapture and *Justin* to sleep. As *Justin* sleeps, *Molly Bloom* approaches, sits at his side, and cradles his head in her arms.]

Enter *Molly Bloom, Achilles, Laura,* and *Keats.*

Achilles: *Très bien*, Virgil! That was beautiful! Please do tell how you create such poetic beauty!

Virgil: [Bated breath of citron rye, mint fennel, and sun-peeled clove.] I was simply caught in the moment, and drawing from my inspiration, I was able to craft my lines. It also helps to call on the powers of the divine muses.

Dante: But of course!

Achilles: Of course!

[*Keats* sits on the lap of *Laura*, with a gentle hand reciting poetry.]

Keats: [*If poetry comes not as naturally as the Leaves to a tree (the
                  bloom, the bloom, whose petals nipped before they blew / died on
                  the promise of the fruit), it had better not come at all.* Suddenly!]

                  But to this lyrical circle of sad hell,
                  Where 'mid the gust, the whirlwind, and the flaw
                  Of rain and hail-stones, lovers need not tell
                  Their sorrows. Pale were the sweet lips I saw,
                  Pale were the lips I kiss'd, and fair the form
                  I floated with, about that melancholy storm…

[All characters, except for *Justin* still dreaming, applaud. *Justin* lets out a
grunt.]

All: [Together in rapture.] Absolutely splendid!

Justin: [Awakens from the applause, finding his head cradled against
                  Molly's breasts.] What's going on? What did I miss? Why am
                  I—?

[His attempt to grab hold of the situation gets cut short as *Molly* places
her hand in gesture, lips in stride against—yes as well him as another
yes I believe I shall Yes.]

All: [Except for her.] Poetry! You missed poetry!

[*Justin* lets out a muffled grunt, as *Molly* again—]

Dante: [Coughs.] I believe it's your turn to come up with something.

Justin: [Breaks away to glare at *Dante*.] And why would I do that?

Dante: We're all doing it. Aren't you a poet?

Justin: [Stands and dusts himself off, trying not to draw attention to
                his—] Unfortunately.

Virgil: There was no greater honor in the arts during my era than to be
                considered a great poet.

Dante: Mine too. In fact, it was considered quite noble.

Justin: Well, I hate to burst your rhyme and metered bubble, but
                nowadays, you tell someone you're a poet, and they assume
                you're a little... [Tilts his head to the side, eyes don the *look*.] off.

Keats: So why do you write then?

Justin: [Reverts back to poet.] Because I'm depressed. And I actually
                love how ignoble poetry has become. It gives me a medium to
                depict the grief I carry.

Keats: Recite to us your grief then.

Justin: I can't.

Keats: Why? We all did.

Justin: Because I don't like talking about it. Just like how I don't
                particularly enjoy discussing poetry.

                [*A Pause* plays flat, thick-hanging in the air, as *Keats* rubs his temples,
                exasperated. *Virgil* and *Dante* shroud in embarrassment.]

Keats: So why are you even here?

                [*Justin* falls silent. All characters except for *Molly Bloom* leave *Justin*
                behind, discussing poetics and process in their wake. *Molly Bloom* sees
                a church in the middle of the field of spectrumed light, and walks in
                leading *Justin* quietly. In the church, there is a two-legged pedestal,
                which *Justin* stands on. He attempts to draw in his surroundings in a
                breath, eyes closed, eyes open, eyes not their own pitch anymore, eyes

two burnt roses, roses two closed eyes opened to ash, opens his mouth,
a dead rose steps out, the breath now rose shaped, carrying a lost
monologue blooming with a silked memory.]

Justin:

Justin wraps himself in word-sewn

shawls and continues

away from the audience,

the backyard pool

where his brother was drowning

once, almost lost in the breathless wake,

into the deep end of it, the shimmer

of all the lemon trees

in our desert born with a green

jaundice, his impending speech

trying to save him

prone to sunburns

winter shaped, no,

the formless symmetry

of his tongue that isn't working,

while looking directly away from

the repeated sounds of nostalgia

as a beached ocean

remembering where he placed it

within bracketed, staged direction,

the Chorus sings 'Jason, why did you do this?'

He responds with a venoming

of red, a gun, and a fractured eye

almost lost, but I ask again,

how could you do this?

But instead, red meets blue, as yellow beams

oceaning to loss,

to loss, singing with the emptiness of light,

statued in the center of a sinking stage;

when did I become an expression of myself

in a language of silent echoes?

The song ends with the melody

lost in the broken quiet of my reach.

[A rose steps over and plucks *Justin* off the church's stage. *Molly Bloom* smiles an open smile as the words resonate inside her. She goes to lock the church's doors, her mouth armed and legged with taste's caress.]

[Elsewhere, *Dante* and *Keats* are now arguing, as *Keats* has seduced *Laura*, *Dante's* great love.]

Dante: [To *Keats*.] This proves that you have never loved truly.

Keats: How so?

Dante: [Pleading.] Laura, I am here, and not

                in this place I thought I created

                incorrect, now lost, seeing

                you, how this hollow

                is so empty, seeing

                you, how this Hell

                sees me like this,

                Keats, you and your

                odes, so crafted and yet

                here, in this Hell, too

                confident, too sickly

                with growth, how you

                understand that you have won

                over my desires, and therefore

                I have loved more deeply

                because my love is crafted

in defeat, as you hold her,

the loudest gesture

to breathe my loss.

[*Dante* leaps at *Keats* and the two exchange literary blows. *Achilles* steps in, lifting them both by the scruff of their robes.]

Achilles: It seems Justin may have a point. Perhaps poetry can be ignoble.

[*Molly Bloom* and *Justin* are seen lying next to each other in the church, together touched by the light passing through the stained glass.]

Molly: I enjoyed that poem you recited.

[*Justin* is silent.]

[The stained light sighs and color-clouds over them.] I imagined you would be more talkative.

Justin: Why would you think that?

Molly: [Studying him.] Well, I'm free to fantasize, no?

Justin: This is true. That's something that poetry and fantasy have in common: creative license.

[She laughs, while her hand gets lost in the slithering tangles of his hair. *Intimate* glows again. Soft.]

[After, mumbles.] I wrote a play before this.

Molly: Oh? And what happens?

Justin: Characters interact with each other. Literary figures enter and leave, frustrated that they didn't have more lines, or able to take the head of the protagonist.

Molly: Ooh! And who is the protagonist?

Justin: The narrative.

Molly: What is the name of it? I want to read it.

Justin: *A Canvas in Arms.*

Molly: It sounds pretty enough.

Justin: It's not. It's ugly.

[*A Pause* is felt holding onto a ledge, released, fading towards the bottom.]

Molly: If I'm being honest, I don't think that's all to it. What else happens?

[*Molly* rests her head on his chest, staring into his eyes. If his eyes weren't so distant or lost in thought, the scene could be interpreted as romantic. But *Justin* is now caught in the swirling pull of memory. *Molly* traces his lips.]

[With a sly smile.] I'm married, you know.

[*Justin* is silent. The eyes blink twice, flinch, and after, unresponsive. *Molly* gets up, makes some brisk adjustments, and at the door, turns back one last time and smiles.]

You poets, you're all hopeless.

Justin: [As she walks out.] Truer words have yet to be written.

Dante: [Finding the entrance to the church, knocks on the door, seeing *Justin* vulnerable for the first time.] Justin, I want to leave this place.

Justin: [To no one in particular, maybe himself.] No, let's keep going. You know I'm very unhappy, don't you? [Notices *Dante's* swollen left eye.] What the hell happened to you?

Dante: I don't want to talk about it.

Justin: And voilà! My poetics!

[*Justin* gets up, throws on a tunic, and joins *Dante*. *Dante* snaps his fingers as they leave, leaving nothing neither beautiful nor holding still standing in this place.]

Heart's Monologue, Remembered

[*Justin* and *Dante* approach an unmarked passageway, where *Heart* stands guarding, still in steps moving forward in march. Inconsistently beating, shrinking, drawing in breath, folding under the beating, how the head of *Heart* is not in agreement with the rest holding together, drawing in, folds into a shrinking, where left in the past. *Justin* stops, looks back at the last level of Hell, and how it went so poorly written. He pours a bottle out of *Glass*. *Heart* breaks his marching stillness and grabs the bottle from *Justin*. *Heart* drinks. And drinks. *Justin* takes *Glass*, catching the fermented aortic liquid now pooling regurgitated out of *Heart's* many valves. *Justin*, *Glass* to lips, drinks. It's early, but both are upset.]

Justin: [To *Dante* after landing awkwardly.] How did you get here?

Heart: I'm in disagreement with everything!

Dante: Oh, I remember you! And here you are.

Heart: Yes, here I am! Here, I fucking am! And nothing has changed.

Dante: You look glum.

Heart: Well, you look positively medieval!

                   [Drops the bottle with a drunk sense of calm.]

                   I'm sorry
                   that wasn't
                   very funny. Well,
                   that's only natural
                   when one isn't happy.

                                         Enter *Over Here!*.

Over Here!:   Why aren't you happy?

Heart: Clearly, you haven't been paying attention.

Justin: [To himself.] What did you think of that last scene?

Over Here!: [Not listening.] How could I? I just got here. Is this Hell? What did I do? [A pair of hands enter and take hold of *Over Here!*.] Wait! No! What did I do? What could I have possibly done? I just got here! I'll pay attention, I promise! I—

Exit *Over Here!*.

Heart: I don't know why it's so hard for me to—[Searches. Nothing. Starts crying.]

Justin: Nothing has changed. Things keep happening all over again. It keeps building up, the tension, the frustration, the sadness, leading to some grand, breaking event, and then all over again, without change, hoping for something different, insisting that it will be different, but this is probably the fourth time, the fourth version of the same thing, the fourth, and I'm counting the last three times, except the last one was the worst, and I'm rambling [Shaking now, heavy.] because it's so sad, and I'm not sleeping, because there is all these cycles of anxiety hanging over us, limp on a rope, and the phone rings now, and after, everyone is so upset, and it's just the morning, and I don't know how much more of this before we all just… I don't know. I don't know, I don't know, I don't know anymore, I don't know why, I don't know what's left, I don't know how to make it stop, I don't know why I'm here, I don't know what is keeping me here, I don't know how to break it, I don't know what is left to say, I don't know if I said it properly, but I think I meant it when I called him that, told him how small and low he was, practically buried in his own actions. And they all said that they agreed with me, and after our staged intervention (Can you believe it? We had a fucking intervention.), my mom and I got ice cream after his exit settled along with the slammed door. I ordered a white chocolate raspberry milkshake, and I was so proud of myself because I finally addressed something important, and yet nothing changed the next day, except more resentment, and then she broke, but before, calling her a cunt, to my knowledge, the first time, and this wasn't addressed, and now we're here, and he is too, and I can tell that she is breaking again, and he doesn't care, and my first instinct is to leave because now this place is breaking me, and I blame a place now

for my actions, and him being here, all absurd, all beyond
the scope of my words, and I don't know why I'm so afraid of
saying what I mean simply.

[*Heart* picks up the replenished bottle of fermented ink and drinks
hungrily. He staggers over to a ledge, above where *Over Here!* is being
fed to *Stage*. *Heart* drinks and sways. *Stage* opens again, its teeth
salivating. *Heart* bottle-tips (**Ending sounds**).]

[*Justin* goes off to be by himself, curling, the lighting changing
into eyes adjusting to the rhythm of a wakeless sleep. Speaking
to a corner reflecting *The Moon*.] Mom, I love you and there
was this one night after when I came back, when you and I
were talking about it, drinking, and you threatened to do it
again because I was yelling now and laughing, and you picked
up another knife, and I was goading you on because there was
this distance between us now, and I hated everyone close to me,
and you had the knife to your wrist again, and your eyes looked
like mine when we lose ourselves, drinking, angry, laughing,
and I know I am yours, and I know you would've done it again,
because he and I know how to say things that cut since we grew
inside you, a changed shape different now by a knife's thirst,
and I asked where was the ache of my weight you carried when
you told me you wanted to die, and what am I but a hurtful
song, grasping that this part of me is real, that I do terrible
things like him, maybe both worse than each other, growing so
ugly and our fault.

[A shuttered gate of ivory night-rosed in onyx appears and opens.
An applauding pair of hands step out and lead *Justin* inside, where a
sleeping *Freud* and *Chair 2* are waiting.]

Meanwhile...

[*Jason* kicks and
stews, calling out
for help that isn't
listening.]

3 Paintings on the Same Scene that Will Happen Later (A Redacted Letter for Help):

I.
Greetings,

This is Dante. ████████████████████████ █ ████████████
████████ singing ███ to chime ███ in with █████ an ██ inadequate
██████ update. [Chiming.] Help! ██████ All is █. ████████ well! ██████
██ Well?
Are you ██████ nuts? No, lost! We may be ██. ████████ hopelessly
████████ Lost! ███ until … ██████ ; however ███ yes, ████████ lost.
What am I doing █ here? Help! ████████ Which reminds me, ██████████
██

██
██
████████████████████████

And then, ████████████████████████████████
██
████████████████████████████
████████████████████████████████. And that wasn't ████████ even the
████████ worst part! Along our journey, ████████ we encountered
████████ a traveling ████████ orchestra? ~~Lost~~ *Lost* ████████
████████ asked for ████████████ directions. Then ████████
████████ [Suddenly!] ████████████ there was a character
called [redacted]. He flies in ████████ through the canopy! Strange and
████████████ shrill ████████ [sic.] ████████████ blood
curdling ████████ scene. Oh God, help us! We barely managed to escape!
[redacted] ███ lose everything, ████████ except our ████████████
████ hopes of seeing ████████ an ineloquent [redacted] ray of light or end
████████████████████ to this ████████████████
literary ████ everything. ████████ Please. ████ Please. ████
Please. ██████. Please? ████████ Please! Barely holding ████████
on. At least ████████ Justin is [redacted] ████████ finally quiet,
but ████ writing. ██████ Poor [redacted] soul. Now there is a [redacted]
emptiness in ████████ these words. In these words, please understand
████████ their ████████████████████████ meaning █.

Please ████████████!
There is no ████ one left ████
to ████████ laugh.

Enter *An Epistolary Intermission.*

II.

██

██████████!

After all that,
or this,
[re█████████████
███████dac███████
███████████ted!]
maybe I am
too.

III.
Greetings,

This is [redacted], █████████████
the song that bore ████████████
witness to the scene. █████████████████████
Oh God! █████████████
Help! ████████████████████

On writing ████████████████████████████
(what better time to discuss poetics than in the midst of chaos!) ████████████
the successful writer must adhere to these steps:
1) ████████████████████████
2) ███████████████████████████████
3) ███████████████████████
4)   Litany
5) ████████████████
6) ████████████████
…
666) Most importantly, ██████████████████████████████ or else!

In short, █████████████████
the successful writer must ███████████████████
craft the delicate break ██████████████
giving shape to ████████████████

layered breath █████████████
of melodic ██████████
discord ████████████████
creating havoc! ██████████
Or not. █████████████████████
Who knows? I don't. Oh God! ████████████

Now back to the scene where ████████████████████████████
Justin he's ███████████████████████
in Italian, ████████████████
not leading, no, instead ████████████████████████████
now, the path least traveled, ██████████████
slips! ████████████
broken off! breaks ██████████
a silence he isn't reaching ████████████████
for sound, meaning, for safety ██████████
all unnerved morale low ███████████
unnerved by creation ████████████████
creating █████████████████
mixed and molded to his own conflict ████████████
a conflicted song ██████████████
how it sounds descending with the ████████████
offset shades of closure ████████████
not reached, Justin, closing to ██████████
his needs of a violent ending to this ████████████████
help! ████████████████
ME! █████████████
scene ██████████████████.

Again, I stress, ██████████████
morale is low. Please send ████████
████████████████ in the ████████ clowns.

             ████████,
             █████████████

The Mystery of the Disappearing Traveling Orchestra

Character List: [Hears frantic movement inside a locked anvil. Peers inside.] What's this trumpet doing here?

Conductor: *Lasciate ogne speranza, voi ch'entrate!* {Abandon all hope, ye who enter here.}

Character List: Holy hell, what happened here?!

Trumpet (Spirit):   It was terrible! There were talons where the beak should be! So many scales! So many fingerings of the same note! But I think I'm dead! [Sees the corpse inside the anvil as confirmation. Trumpet shrieks above its register (X*b*!), and faints.]

Character List: What's this trombone doing here?

Trombone (Spirit):   [Hysterically float-paces.] It was awful! There were wings sprouting wings spitting feathers where the lips should be! So many of my screams talking to other instruments, while he just slicked back his hair, teeth deep in my mouthpiece and— [Trips over its corpse. The corpse's slide spits out a slurred shrill (Tritone Interval: Red#—>Blue*b*).] No! What a terrible, terrible sound! Oh no! I think I'm dead.

[*The Moon* begins to hum a finale remembered. *Conductor* and *Instruments* exit, ascending towards the sound.]

Exit *Conductor* and *Instrument Spirits* (holding their corpses).

[With the finale finished, a curtain-veil draws over *The Moon*; for a moment, all quiet-still. *Character List* attempts to catch a breath, pulse-steps slowing, until there is a snap of fingers, and suddenly a phonograph appears and begins to play a melodic image. *Character List*, afraid to look, doesn't, seeing instead *The Can* perched on the dead shoulder of a still breathing *Timpani*. *The Can* swoops down and slow steps with a hungry gaze towards *Character List*. He snaps his fingers again, raising the volume on the projecting phonograph. *Character List*, not understanding and with eyes shut, is inescapably shown what happened here; the image volume piercing.]

The Can whispers into the ear
of Trumpet, who nods, grabbing
a knife, slicks back the knife
hairs with a wrist, Trombone has
been drinking, slurring sounds
up and down, a flat 9 over
an unfinished chord, *he called her*
a cunt, why wasn't that in the last
play, it was important, the first
fissures of breaking, this music
box isn't working, so Timpani
grabs Trumpet, asks *what are you doing*
tomorrow? Shaking the sounds out
of the spit valves, Trombone says
you're not even trying, like it's supposed to
make sense, The Can perched on his own
shoulder, whispers how much anger he carries
inside as a created character creating
violence, needing to bear it all out,
so tired of music, sound spatters,
Trombone tired of Trombone,
Trumpet nodding, the wrist, oh god,
the wrist spitting out muted tones
of color, the first thing that's beautiful,
here, I don't know where I am anymore, here,
Timpani wants it all to stop, no one is listening
to Timpani because the music hasn't been
very good for a while now, and the music wants to
stop but The Can keeps whispering, calling it
back, calling it into shape, calling it

out of Trumpet, who is on the floor now,

the pulse is low, heaving, heavy,

Trumpet wants to say something, but too much

anger has been spoken, slicked back, looking like

The Can whispering into the ear of

Timpani, telling Timpani that he is truly

omnipotent and terrible, carrying everything

you are afraid of inside, but somehow

because it is a whisper, the softness of these words

soothing the wild beast, which shouldn't, smiling

The Can smiles, the light goes out, The Can

spreads his wings, The Can bears his anger,

no more than just a whisper in body, but after,

all the instruments with their wrists

slashed, as if a cleaver could sing to them

something simple, all bleeding out

as they watch the music walking away.

[*The Can* looks at a shuddering *Character List*, while picking his teeth with a plectrum. *The Can* spots some letters attempting to crawl away. He pounces, snatching them up. Feeling playfully inspired, he spits on the pages, smearing the ink like an erasure poem. He reads them again, and laughs, as the once frightened language pleading for help now reads as an unmoving, misguided comedy, with a quick aside on a non-existent poetics. He wipes his mouth with them, and folds the sketches into an improvised pocket-square. *The Can* kneels down, finding a cracked musical mirror reflecting a sonata to the wilting *Half-Moon*. After self-inspection, there is no evidence of the violence he committed left on his face except for the smile he wears. The reflection shudders, as *The Can* flies away. *Character List* is wilted sound, shaking.]

Hera, Far From Eden

[*Hera*, tired of holding on, the cyclical nature, the impulse to look away from *Zeus*, *Pluto*, *Neptune*, breaks away from Eden, takes *Shovel* and descends flightless in a shawl of arms. As she leaves, she spots the note pearled over in the cherub's fountain. She reads it, and the smile that forms after, rouged and beating. As she reaches the gate, *The Can* swoops down, still picking his teeth.]

The Can: And where do you think you're going?

Hera: I have to leave.

The Can: Wonderful! And you're exceptionally early!

Hera: What do you—

[*The Can* blinks, and a dark flash washes over her. *The Gate* yawns. *Hera* faints and awakens.]

The Can: [Standing over her.] Are you alright?

Hera: What happened?

The Can: There's no time for that! You're exceptionally early, so get moving! Here. [Hands her a message.] Give this to him when you see him.

Hera: [Memory groggy and limp.] Give this to whom?

The Can: [Recites.] The music hears Hera's heart learning its instruments. [A roar of red, and then a composed smile with teeth.] Oh! And tell him it's regarding his brother! He'll love that! Goodbye! [Flies away while singing.]

What a waste of time
What a waste of time
My suicide with desire's ink-blotted thighs

What a waste of time,
There's no greater crime
My suicide with the dead opaline eyes

My suicide with the curdled stare
My suicide has no hair
What a waste of time

What a waste of time
This is where I forget my line!

[*The Gate* opens. A percussive light, a sun consuming another, a backward hour, a flooding fall, and a pair of hands lead *Hera* away to a room where a sleeping *Freud* is reading *Bloodletting* aloud, consoling a dull *Polaris* and a depressed *Carpe Diem*. She enters unnoticed.]

Character List: [Lost.] I don't know where I am.

Descartes: I think, therefore, I mustn't think. [*Cogito ergo sum* or something.]

Carpe Diem: [Stares into his reflection as a gloomy moon.] What's the point?

Polaris: [Paints *North* with the wrong color.] Where am I?

[*Hera* sees *Justin* seated, talking to an imagined *Chair 1*. A flicker of a flicker of a flicker. The pearled note tugs her forward. She hands him *The Can's* message.]

Justin: [Examines the message.] I can't read this. The letters look like they're trying to devour each other.

Polaris: [Sneaks up from behind.] It says 'Your brother says he loves you, Forever Yours, Can-Can.' It's written in an old, archaic language called 'Violénce.'

Justin: [Contorts a white light into something sharp. *Polaris* scurries away. He's yelling now.] Why would you tell me that! You don't know anything! He's—[He stops as *Hera* takes her seat on *Chair 1*.]

Hera: [Hands fold on lap and crown.] Continue.

Justin: [A pause, harp, and breathe.] He says that he loves you, but then he starts getting darker. I don't know how to explain it. I don't think he has the capacity to love. I don't know whom to blame for that.

Drugs: [Suddenly awake!] You can blame me! Blame me, entirely!

Nox: No! Blame me! Blame me!

[*Hera* silences them with a glance; a silk bloom and rosewater calm again. She looks back at *Justin* and smiles, now remembering the inarticulate eloquence of it.]

Hera: Not everything is bleak.

[*Justin* is silent, but his letter gold glows with a full moon's crescent in her left hand. The chilled warmth cheeks against her palm. She leans in to *Justin*, lips and letter close—*Freud*, now awake, snaps his fingers and presses a large red ACME button for effect, as she is led away violent wind by a pair of dislocated hands.]

Freud: [Eyes ink and fire.] You are too fucking early, my dear! [Shattered nails digging into shattered nails.]

[She is gone again. *Justin* is a snapped note off-key, the pitch not breathing now, eyes closed to this stage. The scene settles again. *Carpe Diem* perches a hand on his shoulder.]

Carpe Diem: [Waning to crescent and sighs.] What's the point?

Polaris: [The depiction of *North* is all wrong.] Where am I?

Freud: [Composes himself, wiping away the dark tint of a violent kiss from his cheek, and adjusts his pants.] This is exactly what I was talking about. Neuroses everywhere!

Oedipus: Where? I want to see.

[*Freud* ignores him, closing his eyes again, as he deftly slips into a repressed memory. *Bloodletting* falls to the floor, the pages and feathers scattering.]

Oedipus: [Picks up the last page and reads.] *My mother commits herself to memory/ plucking her body to stringed frets.* [Plucks *Sight* from *Sockets*.] I love it.

Freud: [Now drowsily swaying on a couch, diagnosing the couch with calloused fingertips.] Yes, truly an inadequate ending.

Couch: I disagree. It was quite an intimate ending. I felt its pulse fading in soft beats.

Polaris: [Joins *Freud* on the couch, pondering.] I don't know what I am doing here.

Oedipus: [Joins them on the couch. *Couch* grows smaller.] I'm worried about Justin though. History tends to repeat itself.

History: [Joins them on the couch.] That's not true. I am infinite. [*Couch* grows infinitely smaller.]

Freud: I agree. History does repeat itself.

History: That's not true! I am infi—

Carpe Diem: If that's true, then what's the point?

Freud: I don't know. But I intuitively believe that we are dealing with some very depressed minds right now. [Stands and waves his fingers off-tempo.] What's our motto everyone? 1-2-3!

All: *Eureka e pluribus catharsis!*

Freud: And what does it mean? 1-2-3!

All: Who knows? I sure don't!

Freud: Excellent!

[At that moment, *Dante* finishes up, zips up his fly, and walks through the door to the room.]

Dante: Hello, good doctor. Am I early?

Freud: Not one second premature! [Goes to *Dante* and dons him with
                a rose-thorned laurel. He whispers, pointing to *Justin*.] He's a
                little off, that one.

Dante: [To *Justin*.] Are you ready?

[*Dante* notices *Justin's* wrists ringing softly with lament.]

                Are you okay?

                                                        [Leaves
                                                        drifting down
                                                        from another
                                                        moon. Hell's

                sky leaves
                falling
                its colors

                                                        behind.]

Freud: [Whistles to *Couch*, who obediently shakes all the other
                characters off and heavy-scampers over. To *Justin*.] Please take a
                seat, let's get started in earnest.

                [To *Dante*.] You may take a seat over there for now. [He points
                to an unstable hole in a red-shifting corner. *Dante* does so. The
                rest of the characters circle around *Freud* and *Justin*.] Now, let's
                begin. [Closes his eyes, and takes a seat on *Chair 2*. He snaps
                his fingers and *Justin* awakens from his emotional stupor.]

Justin: [Finds *Couch* gnawing on his forearm, facing a sleeping *Freud*.]
                This is a terribly strange place.

Chair 2:   Yes, and dangerous! [*Oedipus* is now hanging from a wire
                hanger, humming a discordant memory remembered in this

room.]

Justin: [Knots.] I know, so why do I pursue it? Why am I here? Why am I writing this?

[Both *Freud* and *Chair 2* together—]

Both: Because you are wrong about so many things! [*Oedipus* continues to dangle in memory. A content scream is sung.]

Justin: I don't understand.

Freud: [Checks the spelling of tarot cards.] Black Jack (upside-down 13)! Hit me! [Coughs. Continues.] Again, because you are wrong about so many things.

[*Couch* is now gnawing on all the vowels on a Ouija board, while staring at *Oedipus* meat hungry.]

Justin: Why is it that I'm always wrong?

Freud: [A tea splattering of blood read.] Because you have mother issues.

Chair 2: Yes, mother issues!

Justin: But what about my brother? I hate him.

Chair 2: He's an addict.

Justin: Yes, and I can hate him for it.

Freud: But he's an addict.

Justin: I don't understand.

Freud: You're an addict.

Justin: I am?

Chair 2:   Yes, with a very complex relationship with your mother.

Justin: I love my mother.

Freud: The first step is admitting it.

Justin: It's not like that.

Freud: [Flips through *Bloodletting*.] It isn't?

Justin: No, I don't think you read poetry the way it's intended.

Oedipus: [Stops crying for help.] I love poetry!

Freud: This is a play though.

Justin: It's [Pause.] complex.

Freud: [Drinks a glass of patina wet milk dreams.] No, it's a complex!

Chair 2:   [From below, with a soft, panicking insistence.] Was there a purpose in your mother's suffering?

Justin: I was told that it wasn't anyone's fault but hers.

Freud: [A gust from everywhere surrounding, hot breath.] You are wrong about so many things!

Chair 2:   Was there a purpose in your mother's suffering?

Justin: I was told it stemmed from an overwhelming loneliness. I never use that word, or at least try not to. Hearing it was… difficult.

Oedipus: You are wrong about so many things! You are wrong! You are wrong! Help!

Chair 2:   Was there a purpose in your mother's suffering?

Justin: My brother called her a cunt, and my dad said it was her fault.

Freud: And you? What about you?

Chair 2:   Was there a purpose in your mother's suffering?

[*Couch* suddenly opens. *Justin* falls through. *Dante* is finally engulfed by the unstable hole, joining *Justin* in descent.]

Freud: You are wrong about—!/

Justin: [While descending—All the sharp

                            objects into a single

                            image, her expression,

                            my brother gone.] So many

                            broken things.

[*Freud* waves goodbye as both *Justin* and *Dante* plummet towards the next level.]

[A Sleeping *Freud* Gives a Synopsis of the Play So Far.]

Ladies and Gentlemen of The Audience,

Justin is on a journey through Hell to find his brother. For what purpose, I do not know. I do not know if Hell as a metaphor is adequate, or even a metaphor. Allow me to explain the circumstances inadequately. Jason, Justin's brother, was arrested for a third time. Jason is a drug addict. Allow me to rephrase. Hello, my name is Dr. Sigmund Freud, and Jason is a drug addict. Justin tried to write about Jason's drug addiction when it was cocaine. That was when Jason served his first sentence. The second time, Justin tried writing about Jason's addiction to pills and use of bath salts. Neither of us know what kind, but more recently Justin was shaken at 4 o'clock in the morning by a homeless girl who said she was a bird without a nest (or cage or something along lines comprising a bird nest, or cage), screaming that she was sorry for waking him, but Jason took something, and he was bleeding, and yelling, going crazy. Her words. I have not met the guy, but he seems like a swell kid. So Jason rushes in, apologizing, yelling at her that she was a mistake, and that she didn't know what she was talking about. Jason gets arrested and put in jail for a third time later: charges of stealing artwork. Justin's dad says that Jason was "thrown in the can again," hence the character. Justin remembers visiting Jason in jail in the past. He said once that he liked seeing his brother trapped. I struggle to make sense of that. He was scared and much smaller than everyone else. He has always been smaller. He kept making promises he wouldn't keep, Justin's words. All the characters know now that Jason is addicted to meth. Justin can't recognize him without giving his name away. History repeats itself. This play is repeating itself. I hope this makes sense. I don't know if hope has a place here. No, I don't think hope has a place here.

[*Justin*, While Descending, Trapped in the Memory.]

Justin: So she cuts. So she cuts. So she cuts. I don't know if that's an overwhelming loneliness. I think that is people who you love call you a cunt (cu█t), both inside your body at one point, one in a voice that I too carry somewhere in a room like this one, my father saying that my brother is her fault, but really, his. I think love changes after words buried in our subconscious become unearthed, directed in anger, fear and sadness. And they both knew what to say, so good at saying it. I know my mother really wanted to kill herself, as she says it. I blame my brother mostly, but my mother was driven by what my father said, so she says.

Dante: [Descending with him in unison.] Do you still love them?

Justin: I look at them differently now. I don't know what to say other than that.

Dante: I think you should keep trying.

Justin: Is there more to say?

Dante: I don't know, but I think your writing stems from an overwhelming loneliness now. You're disappointed with the people you love the most. I don't know what to say other than that.

Justin: I do love them. But I've accepted that they are who they are at this point. They are the finished articles of imperfect characters.

[The two descend further, but what separates up from down doesn't matter anymore.]

The Scene for Suicides; or, "*Dante*, when your trees scream, *lo senti?*"

[*Justin* wakes up to find *Arms* carried off to sleep in a forest, a forest, trees screaming, wire-wrapped for impossible shapes, for suicide, stunted, stillborn. *Dante* looks on as he recognizes his version of Hell.]

Dante: I created this/ oh no/ this is mine!

Arms: [Lumbering.] Why?

Dante: I don't know. Subconscious somewhere, possibly.

Arms: This part is the worst.

Justin: [After seeing *Arms*, his creation, a sad look. Remembers 'Enter *Fingers* carrying *Arms* off to sleep in a forest.'] I didn't mean for you to end up here.

[*Arms* says nothing, and instead a blank yawn. A wind howls, no air in it, an empty sound. *Justin* goes off to look at all the bodied trees. *Dante* points out that they are actually souls. This circle, and how it was meant for suicide, and all those souls who threaten to do it. The trees limbed and misaligned like a strange, groved cemetery. *Justin* walks over to the alphabetical designation for his family. There, his mother, a tree, his brother, smaller.]

Dante: [Possessed with knowledge, directing now.] It takes nine months to fruit for the male trees. The female trees are sterile, but grow a ghost fruit that takes three eternities to bloom nothing. There's a word that I'm forgetting that describes this phenomenon. It's in the Bible somewhere. Genesis, maybe.

[*Justin* sees a small apple-that-isn't blossom in a scream. The apple-that-isn't bursts.]

Apple: I should just kill myself.

Justin: Do it.

Apple: I will.

[There is an indifference to suicide, as it happens. The apple-that-isn't seeds, becoming its own tree.]

Dante: Suicide becomes the pollinator. As you can see, decomposition occurs over the skin, its insides ferment, the soil eating away at the soil inside the body, the growth of nothing happens almost instantaneously, and now a tree, as you can see.

[A gust of breath; a snapped forest.]

Adam: [As the tree-that-isn't.] I did it.

[*Arms* takes a cleaver pulled from the lake of frozen fire, and plunges it deep into the heart of *Tree* over and over, right-side-up to upside-down again, while singing *Blue's* forgotten hymn. *Adam* is quiet after, screaming everything he wanted to say while expelled, questioning why he is a tree from an apple, *God* plunging down upon him, as the leaves fall like limbs, words ashen with skin, missing how it was before the setting changed, before all the resentment. *Dante* sprinkles spit from a basket to soothe *Adam* to quiet. The cleaver lifts.]

Justin: Stop.

[The cleaver descends upon the tree. A branch snaps. *Adam* snaps like an arm off. A sandy sap flames touched by air. The cleaver raises a scream from all the others.]

        Stop.

Dante: [Pulls up a sprouting *Bloodletting* and reads a passage.] It says here that he couldn't cope with the guilt after being expelled, so he took a cleaver, and now he's here.

[The cleaver lifts from *Adam's* heart, remembered, descending.]

Justin: [In a voice that copes with guilt.]

[The cleaver stops, as *Arms* turns its attention to *Justin*. *Justin* takes
a step forward and makes the sign of a greater meaning with his
hand along the wrists, leaving behind an open mark tannic red. *Arms*
becomes *Sleep*, *Adam* cradled softly away to make amends with a voice.
Justin steps towards his mother and brother, *Dante* reading to them.
Justin stares at this scene, as it bleeds out to gray, his mother crying, his
brother wrinkled in an ashen, hating smile, staring back as *Justin* holds
the cleaver. There is a ticking of groans soul-snapping with each gust of
quiet. *Justin*, *Jason*, and their mother are all held in one look;

> A look of a night
> deceiving quiet
> and cradled—no,
> whispered light.]

Hera, Diagnosed

[*Justin* paints the conclusion of the last scene still on his hands, still shaking, steps back, a sound, a flight of folded birds away.]

[*Adam,* as another moon now in this Hell, lets out a soft glow. All moons (*Virgil,* an ocean *Styx,* a moon-covered *Beacon, Crescent, Adam*), looking at each other, dusked. *Hera* is led back to *Stage. Freud* is busy on *Chair 2,* examining *Bloodletting* with literary scientific utensils.]

Freud: [Flaccidly depressed.] Ah yes, it's you! You must be my next appointment. And you're on time this time, and not attempting anything too [Examines her with two monocles.] salacious with my other charges.

Hera: [Looks at a disfigured *Stage Direction* pushing her forward.] I guess so.

[*Freud* suddenly raises his hand, signaling for her to wait. *Stage Direction* continues to push. *Freud* mouths the final words of *Bloodletting,* and closes the bounded pages, the walls of past scenes reverberating.]

Freud: [Looks at *Hera,* and then at a coughing *Sundial.*] This is going swimmingly. [Writes this down.]

Hera: [Reclines on a couch, legs crossed. *Freud* sketches this to his own interpretation of her body. She snaps her fingers, and *Freud's* notebook wilts to limp.] I'm supposed to do this for some reason, here with you, on this couch. Honestly, I don't see the point.

Freud: So you don't know?

Hera: Not a clue.

Freud: But I thought all higher beings were omnipotent.

Hera: [Places her palms against her pelvis slowly, rowing up and down. Her palms are placed warmth, her stomach a canvas of clouded tide caught under a brittle birdsong.] Some are impotent.

Freud: [Reclines on *Chair 2*. Writes what he sees down.] Oh, what did I call it in Zurich?... Penis envy!

Hera: [No longer listening, completely immersed in the imagined birdsong of a sad melody. In each pulse fragment, *Justin* imagined as folded birds.] Probably.

Freud: [*Freud* seeing a creeping smile spread across her face, snaps his fingers and laughs. The brittle birdsong ends, and with it, all the lives that were. *Hera* still caught in her own fantasy, sees the sun as a dark blinding, as it breaches. *Freud* continues.] Yes! This is clearly a classical case of penis envy. I insist on it. You are a matriarch, at odds with your Grecian husband/brother for supremacy of your equally Grecian family.

Hera: [Her eyes flicker open, showing signs of once glowing.] We disagree on most things, yes. And there was a time when I—well, even intangible things break. And I have been granted power, and because of it, I can do things like become a swan, and play a lute. I can transform into a moon when it sets. Anyway, I was young, and aristocratic, so I got married off quite young to a stranger, who turned out to be my brother. I wish you could've seen everyone's look when I pulled the veil away from his face (he insisted on wearing the veil). Not one ounce of shock, except for mine. It was actually pretty anticlimactic.

Freud: [Dunks his head in an inebriating vat of crushed wings.] There is so much incest and inbreeding, ***slips*** lameness, and infertility, adultery, adulterers, inverted-heroes, adolescence. [For some reason, smirking downward.]

Hera: Maybe that's why I'm here, presently hiding. Maybe I'm depressed.

Freud: And what better place to be depressed than Hell?

[*Hera* shrugs a regal shrug. She remembers a jingle for an ACME Corp. Palm Valley Lakes Rehab Center.]

Chorus: *If you write to cope/ with family or dope/ come here!/ Stay here!/ At least it's not home.* {Standard Package does not include weaning off designer drugs. Generic brands and expired elixirs will be used as substitutes. For the VIP package, please see...}

Freud: I still think this is a classically beautiful case of penis envy.

Hera: [Retorts.] I think it's people like you who created Greco-Roman mythology.

Freud: [Counter-retorts.] Definitely penis envy.

Hera: [Slips on a Freudian minor scale.] I don't think I'm happy.

Freud: Who is?

Hera: I think that's my sin, why I'm here.

Freud: Meaning?

Hera: I want to be happy. I crave it.

Chair 2:   [An uncharacteristic laugh spirals out.] I'm sorry but that's absolutely ridiculous.

Hera: [Again, shrugs.] I know, but what should I do?

Freud: I think you should—

Chair 2:   [Chimes in.] Was there a purpose in your suffering?

Hera: I don't think so.

Chair 2:   Was there a purpose in your suffering?

Hera: I'm just so tired of it all. We all hate each other. We split from heads, we try to eat each other, there are accounts of asexual birth, and one of mine was thrown for an entire day, crippled by the fall, probably here somewhere.

Chair 2:   Was there a—

Hera: And I'm here, trying to hide in the stomach of some penitential being, a Hell in a stomach. My domain is marital union, a clever irony. I hate it, I hate it all; my family, you and your bullshit questions. what purpose is there in suffering? You fucking tell me. We reflect on it so that it doesn't repeat itself, in theory, but it always does. Suffering always repeats itself. That's what I've learned, and that's why I'm here, on this stupid couch that's been gnawing at me this entire time.

[*Hera* gets up, reaches out as a pair of hands, plucks *Justin* from his flightless location, and smothers him in an embrace. *Freud*, in a serious monotone, snaps his fingers, but calmer this time, as *Hera* is transformed into a moon, held by the stem of something glowing with tender.]

Freud: Good, she reached an epiphonic climax. That's how you gain perspective you know, by wading through the nonsense and absurdity to reach repressed intellectual truth. Now she is cursed—I mean cured.

Justin: You mean, you knew?

Freud: Yes, the whole time.

Chair 2:   It was obvious.

Justin: And the bit about penis envy?

[Both *Freud* and *Chair 2* in a murder of coughs. After, *Freud* looks up.]

Freud: She's waiting for you in Eden. Now, it all depends on what you do next.

Confrontation Movement 1

Freud: [To *Justin*.] Are you ready?

Justin: I think so.

Freud: Good.

[*Justin* is brought to a room dark with light too heavy. *Jason* is shown flickering with sleep, murmuring '...ot...uilty,' and their father, with his lips stitched, hands possessed by the urge to break, stumbles forward. The words, 'it's her fault he's like this,' speak, somehow articulate and slurred, but really, meaning how he blames himself.]

And that's not all, folks! [*Freud* unlocks the cage holding *Bloodletting*. It flies over and stands tall in front of *Justin*.] And now, what happens next is up to you.

Bloodletting: [To *Justin*.] Your mother tried to kill herself.

Justin: I know.

Bloodletting: Your mother tried to kill herself.

Justin: [The room begins to fall.] I know.

Bloodletting: Your mother tried to kill herself.

Justin: [The room dissolves into a room into a room into a room.] I know.

Bloodletting: Your mother tried to kill herself.

Justin: [The room opens, its organs and bedding bleeding out to show him.] I know!

Bloodletting: [Close, breathing heavily on him, the taste of copper and his words.] Your mother tried to kill herself.

Justin: Hello!/ My name is Justin/ and my mother tried to/ she tried to kill/ to kill/ to kill/ to kill/ her-/self.

[After *Time* passes, *Justin* digs into his chest and pulls out *The Cleaver*. *Mom* descends from the body of *Shade*.]

Justin goes to his father
looks into his eyes,
and slits his father's wrist
horizontally.

Because of you, because of you,
because of you, because of you...

In this Hell, his father nods.
"I know
and I'm sorry."
[He melts.]

Justin turns violently, bends down,
pouring out, lifting his brother
by the hair, hair still
with sleep, murmuring
"not guilty." *Justin* wants to
tell him so much.

Justin begins shaking with
an overwhelming need
to speak, I need to speak,
BECAUSE OF YOU,
BECAUSE OF YOU,
BECAUSE OF YOU,
BECAUSE OF YOU,
our mother, she...

Justin puts *Cleaver* to
his brother's wrist
vertically. *Justin* puts *Cleaver* to his
brother's wrist vertically. *Justin* puts *Cleaver*
to his brother's wrist vertically. *Mom* watches
Justin. *Mom* is about to
speak, but *The Can*, present, perched on
Bloodletting, gives a piercing

look. *Justin* is shaking. [Words
do not fail me now.]

Cleaver descends. *Justin*,
in this Hell, looks
at himself from
his mother, as he cringes.
The room cringes. *All of Hell*
cringes out of shape.

I carry all of this with me.

In this Hell, *Jason*
is still sleeping.
The Can in his many forms,
not saying anything,
takes *Jason* away, sleep
bleeding away
in a cross, disappointed,
leaving *Justin* in an empty
room stained with
his thoughts to find
his own way back.

The Unquiet After

[*Justin* begins writing on his surroundings, walls possibly, hanged arms
tied at the wrists, gnawing at the noose, gripping for a tighter passage
for air, using his for ink.]

Abandon
> *all hope,*
>> *all who enter*
>>> *here.*

He begins with: I'm sorry, mom, I'm sorry, mom, I want to leave this
place, stuck here, stuck because I am angry, mom, I want to get
past you, what he did to you, him, not me, maybe me, maybe
something we all did that led up to me stuck here, you, your
arms, how they held back, how they flow now, how I ripple,
how these walls creak, how I am sorry by how my shoulders
sink, how I want to save myself from leaving prematurely,
how I sleep, how I don't sleep, all the things that keep me
away from sleep, my thoughts running away with thoughts
of running away, leaving a trail of thoughts behind, probably
contemplating something dark to do to the body, when we least
expect it, after chanting cunt enough times, but his addiction
made him, and his addiction broke everything, but it's not his
fault, so they say, because people are inherently good, so they
say, so it goes, but I disagree with these words, how it is his
fault, how there is a conscious decision involved, how he is
led by his impulses, how that is his fault, how I am wrong for
saying that, but vindicated in my belief that I am right, how
literature wants to tell you, how poetry specifically wants to
tell you, that addiction is okay, and that's not what it is saying,
how I am wrong for bastardizing this interpretation of morality,
how I am here in some chained circle of hell, how it isn't so
simple, because addiction is complicated, and how a part of me
forgives him because I agree with poetry, how the other half
prefers silence, how the other half tries to chain away poetry,
tries to look at behavior objectively, how I can't empathize with
a drug addict, how at one point guns were involved when they
didn't need to be, what didn't we provide objectively, how he
feels sorry for himself, how I feel sorry for myself, how we all
feel sorry for ourselves, because we are a family of artists, how
we are a family without art, how we try to kill ourselves in

plain sight, how we keep our secrets softly, how I want to get away, hide in my sleep, but unable to say what I mean, to say that I am sorry, to say that I love everyone with a grain of salt, how nothing changes, how things changed after, what I don't have to tell you, because you already know, because I have failed as a writer, as I believed too much in poetry, not enough in simple imagery, concise words, here I will leave you, here I will feign knowing what to do to end this, here I will make my final bow.

[Takes a chandelier of blood, and places it to his wrist, deep enough.]

Elsewhere...

[A cloaked figure enters Eden, carrying a waterfalling door. The door struggles, so *The Cloaked Figure* sets it down, and shuts it, and Eden, in a flash of color, becomes nothing. All moons are gone now, made to leave. *The Cloaked Figure* lies on the floor, the sound of warm water running, the door closed, the quiet sound a slow cut makes, bleeding out. The door opens, and *The Can* steps out, emptiness and abyss behind, and flies to *Hera*.]

Hera: [Being pushed towards *Exit* by a disfigured *Stage Direction*.] No, stop! I don't want to leave. I'm waiting for Justin.

The Can: Justin isn't coming. He failed, and now he must be punished.

Hera: What do you mean?

The Can: He reenacted Greek Tragedy.

Hera: [Mortified!] He didn't!

The Can: He did. He took a chandelier and tried to kill himself.

Hera: He didn't!

The Can: He did. He tried to kill his father with his brother.

Hera: He didn't!

The Can: He did. He sat on the floor feeling sorry for himself, while his mother watched.

Hera: He didn't... [*The Can* waves his hand over *Hera's* eyes, a flash, and *Hera* sees the scene where *Justin* confronts his father and brother, with his mother watching. She passes out and later awakens to find herself seated on her own throne in a new garden, in a new play. The pearled note is gone. In its place, a brush and a canvas. *The Can* emits a quiet sad-light, spreads his wings and departs.]

The Intermission-Exorcism of *The Devil in Plaid* (Revisited)

[*The Devil in Plaid*, self-chained to the frozen fire, listens with the overtures escaping.]

Justin: Here I am.

Devil: What an odd thing to say.

Justin: [Attempts to wipe the heaviness from his eyes, dangling now.] Stranger things have been said.

Devil: You know, I could free myself at any time if I wanted to. [Snaps his fingers, and a dud shakes *All of Hell*. He looks perturbed.] That wasn't supposed to happen.

Justin: I don't think I'm supposed to leave yet.

Devil: [Tugging at his chains, snaps his fingers, and the dud becomes a parade of colors. *All of Hell* blossoms into a buried fragrance, shaking and settling into dust. Again, he looks perturbed, still chained.] That wasn't supposed to happen!

Justin: Do you mind not snapping your fingers while I think?

Devil: Apologies, my dear character. [Snaps his fingers, and the dud echoes a sharp cry for help in blue amethyst. Still chained, relents.] That wasn't supposed to happen… I give up. [Snaps his fingers. Nothing this time.]

Justin: Maybe it's better that way.

Devil: Do you not remember me?

Justin: It's too dark to remember.

Devil: But it's me!

Justin: You're bound to be someone.

Devil: Yes, yes, but really, it's me, the Devil.

Justin: [Remembering the voice of the snapped fingers.] Are you still wearing that corset?

Devil: You mean the plaid one?

Justin: Yes, that one.

Devil: [Smirking a sinful smirk.] I'm not telling :)

Justin: [Snaps his fingers, and *Eyes* shine to reveal eyes staring back, blank and dead, smiling a glint of what once was. The room is lit now for some reason.] Where are you? [The frozen fire is empty in chains.]

Devil: [Crouching behind, reaches and snaps his fingers behind *Justin's* ear. *Justin* screams. *The Devil* mimicking a forgotten scene.] 'Virgil what do I do?' [Laughs a catastrophic dud.] You see? You were wrong to think I was chained.

Justin: [Turning around, facing the embodiment of the frozen fire.] You're even plaider.

Devil: [Twirls, mimicking a forgotten twirl.] In what layer of Hell do you now reside?

Justin: [Snaps. Just a sound tries to breach, falls to drown in a swamp bed of strings.] The one where I'm supposed to bury my choices leading up to this conversation, get up, persevere somehow for your pleasure, and confront the conclusion.

Devil: Nope. You're in the intermission circle, where you get to assess what you want from the play now. You get to take into account progress, perseverance, and maybe even absolution.

[*Justin* becomes a Hellish apocalyptic scene, where his sky splits, thoughts crawl out, arms, and then legs. His sky splits into a head, his head, smiling for some reason, words now cloaked, false words, the anti-words counting.]

Justin: [Counting all the horses in a burning field.] 1st Conquest, 2nd

War, 3rd Famine, 4th Death—

Devil: [Continues after streaking his hand across the failed apocalyptic scene.] 5th Truth (as an augmented triad), 6th Forgiveness (in second inversion), 7th Ottoman the Fainting Couch, 8th Yoo hoo!, 9th Mentor, 10th Penance, 11th Patience, 12th Patients, 13th 13, 14th Freud, 15th CSPAN, 16th Deus Ex Poetica, 17th Humbert H. Dilemma, 18th Lolita 'Lollipop' Intervention, 19th Godot, 20th Cliffhanger Closure, and the final one is off orchestrating events for a play.

Justin: [Curled in a shattered, fetal crystal sonnet.] My mom had a horse named Blossom. One eye was blue, the other brown. One told the present in brown, the other spoke of blue. Blossom died from a hoof infection. There was a time before, when she got gout from overeating apples. My mother loved that horse. My brother messaged her shortly after she died saying he hoped Blossom was burning in that field over there.

Devil: [Points to a field in Hell.] You mean her?

[*Blossom* is seen wrapped in a limply hanging water halo, enveloped in this scene, but untouched by the fire. She is safe here, but dead still. I'm sorry.]

Anyway, I'm off to bed. Figure out what you want. [Cuts through his corset of words, his finger sliding down, something sharp extended. An angelic darkness is loosed, the sides, the stomach, crippled wings; all that was this character. Steps into the bristling frozen fire, and re-clasps his chains, looks to *Justin*, snaps his fingers, and *The Can* from below appears.]

Enter *The Can*.

[*The Can* smiles an apocalyptic scene glinting.]

[*The Devil* claps.] My final horseman.

[*The Can* with one eye brown, the other blue, picks up *The Devil* and cradles him clasped in sleep.]

Justin:	[Patting *Blossom* now, not paying attention to the chaos behind him. But *The Audience* sees. *The Can* and *The Devil* makeshift something sacrificial to be shorn. How it will scream and unfold, ticking a dumb smile in the fire, and after, to return to the same painful place to repeat.] I'm sorry. [*I'm Sorry* is thrown into the flames by a tarnished, hooved *Patience. The Can* wrings a smile, *The Devil's* shadow clawing into a plaid *Confession Booth. Blossom* dead canters *Justin* inside graceless.]
Devil:	[His tongue slithering silver again.] Hello again, my child. [In a familiar voice.] Tell me that you love me.
Justin:	I confess that I love you. [*Justin*, from his temples, sprouts a pair of French horns. He doesn't know how to play them, looking the part in this place though.]
Devil:	Now tell me what troubles you.
Justin:	[Feeling his horns, a tremor heard through the fingerings.] I thought you were sleeping.
Devil:	I still am.
Justin:	I think my brother is going to die a self-inflicted death. I have a feeling.
Devil:	How does that make you feel?
Justin:	I confess that part of me hates him.
Devil:	Why do you hate him?
Justin:	[After confessing an empty feeling.] My mother didn't change out of her riding clothes for three days after her horse died. She said she could still smell her in the fabric. She was a mess, and my brother sent her that message, and you could hear it in her voice (hear it in her voice, the infinite notes and measures of sadness). [Pauses.] But she still loves him. She still fucking loves him. [Pauses again. Longer this time. A moon rises and sets.] I don't know how to express that more eloquently.

Devil: [Struck by the sentiment. A forgotten written line of loving someone remembered. Gestures and conjures something sharp.] Here, take this.

[*The Devil* passes a syringe full of alphabet soup over to *Justin* through the confession slot.]

Justin: [Looks at the syringe.] What is it?

Devil: Fraternal perspective. [Points to the horns.] Your instruments have been quiet, correct?

[*Justin* attempts sound. Nothing.]

                See? Come on! It's a play! What's the worst that could happen? Your character getting killed off? You'd just end up back here with me. Now quit dawdling! [Academically.] *Equi donati dentes non inspiciuntur.*

[*Justin* considers it, and after a while, digs deeply with the needle, and pushes the plunger down slowly, the consonants and vowels organized in ill-fitting lines. The needle gets taken away. *The French Horns* begin to sound and melody sway.]

French Horns: [As an articulate instrument.]

                'And here I am

                breaking something quiet

                swaying out

                for you {echo}.'

Devil: [Smiles, appreciating his handiwork.] And finally, let these be my parting words to you. [*The Devil* plants a kiss and a forgiving symbol. Three measures and a coda later, *The Can* swoops down on the offbeat, digging into *The Devil's* side. The skin opens. A rib is taloned free. *The Can* bows and presents the rib to *The Devil*. He nods and snaps his fingers. The rib sparks, burns, and brimstones into a tilted organ. *The Can* catches a fainting *Devil* collapsed but still humming the melody invoked from *French Horns*. *The Can* snaps his fingers and departs with *The Devil* asleep in his arms, while everything gets pulled from their roots and ushered away. The scene ends in an open, unresolved blue passage where *Justin* grieves with his notes and instruments.]

The Devil in Plaid, now *Lucifer, Remembered Wing-Suited & Gold Shadowed*

Lucifer: [Floating on a calm surface elsewhere, later in time, looking up smiling, feeling the tender outline of an organ-shaped hole from his left side.] I did something good again. [A sun beams back as he wades in a pool of opaline major scales, as *Justin's* ending song plays from the sky.]

Chorus' **Monologue**

[In the quiet, a tilted organ is played by *Justin*, still French Horned and cloven. *The Organ* sings *Blue's* Bergamot Arabesque (second rouged movement). *The French Horns* play a forgotten watercolored field over the melody, along with an imagined *Voice from Above* descending ascending scales. *Justin* continues drifting through the keys and pedals, phantom bodies escaping out from the false-chords, taking shape behind him as *Chorus*.]

Chorus: [First, slow and soft, like a voice beneath a whisper.] There is no love for you here. [The unheard whisper-song faints to background. The ripple settles. Silence. A second whisper breaches.] There is no love for you here. There is no love for you here. [Silence after settling.] There is no love for you here. There is no love for you here. There is no love... [The mantra and momentum grows. *Chorus* takes a sharpened flat 9 to a muted silhouette; an audible wound.] There is no love for you here. There is no love for you here. There is no love for you here. There is no love for you here. There is no love for you here. There is no love for you here. There is no love for you here [*Chorus* as a frantic body of harmonic dissonance suspends the 2 (sus2) over something bottomless. The vocal body reaches limp for it, as the pitch drops.]... there is no love for you here there is no love for you here there is no love for you here there is no love for you here there is no love for you here there is no love for you here there is no love for you here there is no love for you here there is no love for you here [*Chorus* builds upon itself, the mantra overlapping, volume clawing past articulation. More More More. *Justin* still as the disappearing *Melody* approaching.] THERE IS NO LOVE FOR YOU HERE there is no love for you here THERE IS NO LOVE FOR YOU HERE there is no love for you here [Closer and closer, almost strangling near.] there is no love for you here [Choking the mouth open.] there is no love for you here, there is no love for you here, there is no love for you here, there is no love for you here, [Maybe if I set them to something sharp, maybe if I set them to something sharp, maybe if I set them to something sharp.] there is no love for you here [The suspended 2 curses *Chorus* to repeat this until it never ends.]...

[*Voice*, still in silence, fades to background, climbing above the rafters.]

Carpe Diem: When I get depressed, I take the air away and see the music wilt.

Pandora: When I get depressed, I curl up like a faint line listening to a curdled sound.

Carpe Diem: When I get depressed, I make lists from my breathing ashes.

Pandora: When I get depressed, I cross out the violent scents with night's slit edge.

Carpe Diem: When I get depressed, I see my words wrong, dropping like limbs.

Pandora: When I get depressed, I keep mine cavitied and wrung in an amethyst mouth.

Carpe Diem: When I get depressed, I feel sorry for myself looking back at its hungry reflection.

Pandora: When I get depressed, the reflection becomes the flesh of a starved smile.

Carpe Diem: When I get depressed, I start forgetting that there is a fire singing singed-tender against my neck.

Pandora: When I get depressed, I hatch the ocean as a burning marital bed.

Carpe Diem: When I get depressed, I marionette the air away and watch the moon faint blue.

Pandora: When I get depressed, I leave blue as a sound twitched nightscape falling towards its dawn.

Carpe Diem: When I get depressed, I quartz the cannibal back in the basement.

Pandora: When I get depressed, I quarter the hunger of the cannibal's grip.

Carpe Diem: When I get depressed, the unlocked moon pours out, back and
               forth.

Pandora: When I get depressed, I set the moon on its children.

               [Both pausing, drawing their next words in a synced breath.]

Carpe Diem: [Remembering.] When I get depressed, I open the locked box
               with a cleaver.

Pandora: [Remembering.] When I get depressed, I feed the locked box
               the limbs of its contents.

[From the mouth of the unlocked box, now hacked open and fed,
a written body crawls out, climbing to its legs. Standing before all,
Bloodletting, for the nth time, bows as the poetry. *Voice from Above the
Rafters* plummets back to stage. *Bloodletting* strips *Voice* of its mask,
tender tender tenderly, revealing *Dialogue*. Water light and a somber
Melody, as they embrace. *Melody* opens. *Dante* enters, and grabs *Justin's*
hand. Exit through *Melody*.]

Day 1 (10:00 am Appointment)

[*Dante* and *Justin* walk through a doorway revealing *Freud* again seated on *Chair 2*. *Freud* is scribbling away and asleep with a sharp and extended scientific device peering into *Chair 2's* dreams. There are birds swooping contoured in an inelegant display of rose-quartz flightlessness. A quiet *Chorus* is offstage bird-watching, while *Chair 1* mopes sprawled on the floor after attempting to join in flight, but taking to it like the ground.]

Dante: Hello, good doctor. [Points to *Justin*.] I brought the patient you requested.

[*Justin* looks uncomfortable. *Freud* sits cross-legged with the gravity of some morose relic or demi-figure.]

Freud: [Annoyed.] What patient? [Studies *Justin* for awhile.] Ah, yes, hello again, and greetings. Allow me to reintroduce myself formally; I am Freud, the demigod of thought, irrationality, and psychosis. [Checks the schedule trying to escape.] Pleased to finally and formally make your acquaintance at your appointed time. Now, if you'll take a seat, we can begin.

Justin: [To *Dante*.] Is this really necessary? I really didn't want to come back to this place.

Dante: I had to do this too. I didn't write about it, but I believe I met Freud during the *Intermezzo* between greed and wrath. I think all great works go through Freud at some level.

Freud: Well said. And with that, [Snaps his fingers.] I relinquish you of your trial.

Dante: You mean I'm free to go?

Freud: No, but you can take a seat in the corner over there and be quiet.

[*Dante* does so.]

Justin: Wait, wait, wait... This is a sequel, and I didn't do this for my last play. [Suddenly, an imagined *Memory* reveals *Chair 1* as the

Chair from *Bloodletting. Justin* remembers now.] Oh God! It's you!

[*Memory* exits, caress-forgotten away in the arms of *Amnesia.*]

Chair 1:   [Still folded as a chair-swan.] Yes, it is I, the semi-demi-god Chair 1 the (Con)Seated.

Justin: That's the Chair who kept drooling while asking me about my mother's suffering from before! [Lunges at *Chair 1*, but *Freud* snaps his fingers, and *Justin* is restrained by a pair of hands. After struggling for a bit, Justin turns his attention to *Freud* with a rabid glare.] So where were you?

Freud: Fool! I was invisible! I was the music listening in on the dialogue.

Justin: [Unknots himself from the hands.] That's a cop-out.

Freud: [Writes that down.] Why yes, a literary cop-out! But let me ask you this; who do you think sent that dumb, poor excuse of a stool over there? [Pointing to *Chair 1*, gnawing on one if its legs.] Did it just... appear? Why, of course not! I sent the chair as my messenger and you spoke to it like a good little boy. Now, if you don't mind, let's begin. I charge by the hour.

Justin: No, I believe I shall be going. Where is the exit?

[A flash of light dulls in annoyance. *Freud* snaps his fingers, and the pair of hands strap *Justin* into a wobble-standing *Chair 1*, spitting pearls again.]

Freud: Trust me; I'm a very good listener.

Justin: [Silent.] I'm fine though.

Freud: Let me pose a question, if I may. You consider yourself a poet, yes?

Justin: No.

[*Chair 1* subtly flaps, attempting a quiet swan-dive. *Freud* flicks *Chair 1* on the cheek.]

Freud: [Sternly to the chair.] Settle down stool. [All light quivers for a moment. Sight is unseen. *Freud* checks on *Chair 2's* dream measurements, and then returns his attention back to *Justin.*] Well, let me pose this question anyway. The poet John Berryman once said, {Conceives the voice of John Berryman} *The artist is extremely lucky who is presented with the worst possible ordeal which will not actually kill him. At that point, he's in business.* Do you believe you have to be suffering in order to produce good art?

Justin: And how do you quantify 'good art?'

Freud: Let me ask the questions here, if you don't mind.

Justin: Fine. John Berryman jumped off a bridge, so he must have been pretty unhappy. He was also a Confessionalist.

Freud: Again, I charge by the hour, so if you don't mind, I would rather you not give me a biography on the man.

Justin: [At some point, the arms tying *Justin* to the chair let go. *Justin* picks up a quiet guitar and starts plucking some notes into origami sounds. The guitar becomes pearled.] I'm trying not to deflect so much anymore. I think that is one of the issues of surrealism, which I attribute my poetics to. Surrealism prioritizes image over content, but the imagery can be so damn beautiful and twisted. But yes, trauma is essential. And surrealism can be the perfect medium for deflecting trauma, because the reader often forgets that *Ceci n'est pas une pipe,* you know? Poetry relies on imagery and there is a certain treachery of images.

Freud: If I may interject here… actually, I forgot what I was going to say. Anyway, continue please. Wait, no! [Pause.] Never mind. Please continue.

[*Justin* plays a suite with the rasping mutes of trauma. The staccato

of beating bird wings heard spindled to a string-flutter of snapped
red. There is a bloom of scented light humming to the quiet parts of
this song. The chiming of a forgotten memory buried in the flames
of a damp fire in the locked attic. The lock is a pearl, and the key an
unfinished painting of an unhinged moon strapped to the emptiness
behind it. These are all missing notes on the guitar *Justin* is gripping too
tight. *Justin* is formed to words, but catches a breath in mid-flight. The
breath produces an egg. The egg hatches a body without wings and flies
away, back to staccato.]

Justin: I don't think the poet can be mentally stable. That takes
             away all credibility of the artist. Our task is to reach within our
             subconscious. I believe that takes a toll on one's perception of
             reality. Our reality eventually becomes poetry. That is a decision
             the artist must make.

Freud: That seems fair enough. But going back to trauma…

Justin: I'm getting to that. So we dig, and dig, traversing deeper
             into ourselves. I think that is what separates surrealists from
             other aesthetics: the rejection of what the eye shows us,
             pursuing a truer image hiding within the subconscious. But it
             takes trauma to draw you away unwillingly past the eye's image
             and into consciousness' throat within yourself, a dissonant
             siren call, as generally, the image is an unbalanced reflection of
             the surrealist's voice. But then this is where I feel quite a few
             surrealist poets fall short; if trauma allows you to access that
             part of your subconscious, then the next step is to then shift
             the imagery back to trauma. Surrealism obscures perception
             to create an image that is unique, but it oftentimes fails to risk
             anything other than its uniqueness. Surrealism warps image,
             but successively unsuccessful surreal poems are not saying
             anything legible but it's sung by a painted voice, so then the
             image becomes *idée obscura*: full-spectrumed but not satiating.
             This is where I believe Confessional Poetry comes into the
             fold. Confessional Poetry gives the poem context, that its
             understanding by the reader is important, that revelation, and
             therefore pathos, are needed for the Confessional Poem to be
             affecting. Trauma shapes the poet, but oftentimes the surrealist
             fails at shaping the poem into art that is eloquently vulnerable,

wound-open and deranged. Otherwise, what is the point? I want to paint surrealism in the colors of pathos. I believe in that image.

Freud:
But from what I understand, you didn't experience something truly horrific until after you started writing, correct? And also, you're suggesting that a surrealist poem needs to explicitly evoke pathos. But the foundation of surrealism is interpretation, not so much understanding. The elusiveness of the image can also be beautiful, no?

Justin:
I was always unhappy to varying degrees. But I think I lost my metaphorical marbles after my mother tried to kill herself. And I know there is no 'end-all, be-all' to poetry. And I stress that I know just as much if not more than any wise man. [I know that I know *ipse se nihil scire id unum sciat.*] And this isn't supposed to be some far-reaching manifesto. I say this with absolute sincerity; who the hell am I to say, 'A poem must do [this or that]!' In this moment, all I really want to do is to let you in on what I'm aiming to do in this play, that I need you to understand. Beyond that, the whole premise of a manifesto is so narcissistic. I read this one manifesto written by a neo-anti-shapist who said that if the reader and/or audience can imagine an image, then the poem has failed. Doesn't that just make you want to lock yourself up in some remote hole and reaffirm your commitment to the written word? [He considers it, *Time* eclipses, and then *Justin* returns, digging himself out of the cushioning of *Chair 2. Chair 2* lets out a grunt, blinks, *I've been slain!,* and returns back to its dream. *Freud's* scientific instruments continue to monitor. *Justin* takes his seat again on *Chair 1.*] I forgot to ask if this conversation is confidential.

Freud:
[Laughs.] Confidential? Of course not! [At the last second, reconsiders during the climax of falling from a tender bridge. He dusts off the fall after sitting back down.] I think I'll be the judge of your insanity, and let me just say that depression doesn't necessarily lead to insanity. That's in most cases anyway, or at least I think. Try to hold it together [Fragments into a subconscious desire.], will you? [A stern yawn.] Now, if you'll get to my second point about the importance of interpretation

in relation to surrealism.

Justin: Yes, interpretation is important, and I agree that the beauty of
               surrealism is that it allows room for the reader to attribute their
               own meaning to it. And that is all well and good. But that
               isn't what I want this play to do. I want to express something
               traumatic to you with the language I've been given by my
               trauma.

Freud: Placing ownership with trauma seems kind of superficial, if
               you were to ask me. Saying things like, "My trauma
               traumatized me and *poof!* gave me language" just hits the ear
               wrong. [Rubs the lobes of his temples to try to quiet them.]
               Except for the *poof!* part. I'm okay with onomatopoeia.

Justin: [Quiet for a while until it passes and then honestly.] I disagree.
               Maybe the melody is wrong, and worse, not even a melody, but
               I think it's actually empowering. Or else what is the point? I
               didn't want to talk about it. I kept it close for so long, without
               ever wanting to reveal it to anyone. And it just wore me down,
               holding something so heavy. [Grief is shaped into a heavy
               feather.] But still, I couldn't talk about it. I would mumble
               through certain passages, stumble with the beginning, and then
               stop. I'm truly not that articulate. So I decide to write about
               it? How does that make any sense? What's wrong with me?
               [Shaking.] The whole impulse to create from something dark
               just seems so… bizarre. [Pause.] But then it happens.

Freud: [No, nothing to see here, folks.] Then what happens exactly?

Justin: [Opens his chest, and *Heart* hands him a copy of *Bloodletting*.]
               This. [Smiles, beaconing a pale light.]

Freud: And what is that?

Justin: [Again, that smile. Continues to strum through the pages.]
               Articulation.

Freud: So do you think that art can be healing?

Justin: May I paraphrase? "I was a Flower of the mountain yes when
             I put the rose in my hair like the Andalusian girls used or shall
             I wear a red yes and how he kissed me under the Moorish wall
             and I thought well as well him as another… [*Freud*, with all
             the realism that sleep allows, falls in. Wakes in *Eros* descending
             like the universe snow-falling faintly through, the universe
             faintly swooning, descending down to ascension, no, not mad,
             descending faintly like the descent mad and decanted, a pink
             salted pinch, melts the flower with perfumed snow, breathing
             in the fragrant climb bottled for memory, the symbol of gesture
             anyway, his heart beating like the descent of their last end, the
             universe and the body descending into, outside the window,
             snow shines softly across the drifting night, the fingers into a
             necklaced caress, falling upon all the living and the dead.]…
             then he asked me would I yes to say yes my mountain flower
             and first I put my arms around him yes and drew him down
             to me so he could feel my breasts all perfume yes and his heart
             was going like mad and yes I said yes I will Yes."

Freud: That was… [Pause.] Well, anyway, what were we discussing
             again? Oh yes, I remember. So you want this to be a
             Confessional/Surreal play?

Justin: Again, I just feel that there is so much unrealized with the
             Surrealist movement. The primary impulse of a surrealist
             is to strive for the unique, and non-real, which is fine, but
             sometimes it is so easy to deflect. I had—[Drifts, and then the
             return, fall landing.] no, *have* a tendency to deflect. So then the
             image becomes empty. I love the impossible image, but want it
             to carry something! I need it to be more! [Breathes.] Maybe I'm
             not explaining myself properly.

Freud: You're not, I assure you. And you're anti-deflection sentiment
             falls quite flat, considering it's taken you this long to finally see
             me to address your issues. But that's fine, considering I deem
             you [Does so.] insane. And if I'm not mistaken, you previously
             labeled your aesthetic 'absurdism.'

Justin: I wanted [An absurd image bobbles.] to laugh.

Freud: [Laughs.] So now you are in the pursuit of watering down surrealism. That's rich.

Justin: [Shrugs.] That's fine; then I'm an absurd, watered-down surrealist.

Freud: [Breaks the silence by making a loud, forgiving symbol in the air.] Well, our time is up for today. But I'll leave you with this quote: "We must not fear daylight just because it almost always illuminates a miserable world."

Justin: And what do you suppose that means?

[*Freud* snaps his fingers, and *Justin* is restrained and taken to the padded room again, where he is locked into a straightjacket stitched with all the off-silhouette expressions of insanity. *Freud* digs into an imagined chest pocket and tosses him a notebook and an empty pen.]

                What the hell am I supposed to do with that? [He makes an unbalanced look that tilts with the assuredness of confusion.] I'm a little tied down.

Freud: [*Freud* laughs, bids adieu, and locks the door behind him, but before—] That's the proper attire for this aesthetic, no? Or am I crazy?

[*Time* passes.]

[*Time* Passes.]

[*Time* paces in circles around *Justin*, who is still-houred and quiet, coiled in the heavy knotted breath of his straightjacket. *Time* twitch-ticks away as *Justin's* surroundings shift into imagined percussive snaps from violent strings and the emptiness of white space. *Time* flees as the white-space cracks open, lips parted, a mouth revealing all the teeth and tongues of a tasting black hole. The notebook *Freud* left him shrinking violet, stem and flower, pages wavering wordless in the reverse gust of an empty wind. From the mouthing black-hole steps out a shaded *Sundial* wick-flickering an incorrect *Time*. The dark-hole closes, resuming its pose as white-space again. *The Sundial* steps forward, and directs a plummeting sun to sink; the painted song of the after-emptiness of light crackling in a dark fire. A string snaps to voice. *The Sundial*, with its act complete, dissolves into lunar seconds. All light and melody soured to quiet. *Justin* continues to glare, eyes humming rhythmic and distant at the empty notebook.]

Day 666 (4:45 am Appointment)

[*Time* seasons past the room, scared to encounter white-space again. Eventually though, *Time* builds up its courage and enters *Justin's* room. But upon doing so, *Time* trips over the neglected notebook, looking dehydrated and malnourished. Suddenly, a fanfare of shrieking instruments brass note their calls for attention. *Freud* enters rhinestoned in ring leader garb marching with a baton over the fallen *Time, Polaris,* and *Carpe Diem* following in syncopated steps glumly behind. *Polaris* shakes *Justin* awake. *Justin* checks the risen *Sundial*, which reveals it's 4:45 am. *Freud* directs the straightjacket to tighten, and it does so, cutting off all circulation. *Chair 3* and *Couch 1* are introduced in an atonal melody to accommodate the extra bodies. *Freud* takes his seat, lounging on *Couch. Couch* is confident, pearl-necklaced and draped in a *Roman* wreath, blanketed with a conqueror's red tapestry. *Justin* is planted on *Chair 3*, who wobbles threadbare and nervous. *Chair 3* is floral patterned in winter, warmed with the gray from a frozen ocean. *Polaris* and *Carpe Diem* take their seats on *Chairs 1* and *2*, both vomiting pearls after contracting a pearl virus. *The Moon* dawns in the room. *Couch* takes a sip of nacre in a pearled cup. The pupils of the new moon dilate. *The Sundial* nightshades to violet, as the incorrect time approaches an alarmed hour. *A Finger* draws to tongue tasting the scent of nightrose blooming as it wilts. *Chairs 1* and *2* Greco arm-wrestle, which escalates to new heights of purple and red. No winner is crowned as the victor's calf is felled. *Couch* leisurely snacks, nibbling on still-beating chair-pegs. *Freud* passes a note along to someone who isn't there, instructing the room to get set to broil. The characters take their seats, the seats take their characters, and the room becomes an oven.]

Freud: Hello everyone.

Chairs: Hello doctor!

Couch: [Half-chewed chair-pegs and spittle spindling out.] Hello doctor!

Room: [Laced lips vibrating seduction.] Hello, good doctor.

Justin: [Under his breath.] Brown-nosing suck-ups.

[*Freud* glares at *Justin*.]

Freud: So? How's the writing going?

Justin: [Still in the straightjacket.] Not well.

Carpe Diem: Not well.

Freud: [Laughs.] Ah yes, the two lyrical vomitons.

Chair 2:   You made that up, didn't you?

Freud: More precisely, I dreamt it. You see, I had the most horrid
                  dream where I was in a session with Justin, and he just kept
                  going on and on about trauma and surrealism. And in my
                  dream, I thought, "Wow, this guy thinks he's some kind of
                  walking manifesto. What a vomit-on. And then I threw a
                  notebook at him to shut him up, but at that point, he was
                  already in a straightjacket." [Bundles over from laughing.]

        [*Justin* and *Carpe Diem* stare at each other.]

Justin: [To *Carpe Diem.*] You write?

Carpe Diem: Not well, as I mentioned.

Justin: May I see your work?

        [*Carpe Diem* shows *Justin* a bursting notebook.]

Freud: I see you've taken to your diary!

Justin: [After reading.] Wow, this is really depressing!

Carpe Diem: Yeah, well, I'm depressed. That's why I'm here.

Justin: I don't know why I'm here. I'm supposed to be on a journey
                  through Hell for some reason and then I ended up here.

        [*Polaris* wakes from a dream.]

Polaris: You mean you haven't figured it out yet? Where do you think

	you are?
Justin:	I'm not sure. It looks like some kind of psychiatric facility.
Carpe Diem:	But the room spoke. That's not normal. I think you might be depressed, too.
Freud:	Absolutely. My dear fellow, you are unequivocally and without a shred of doubt [Doubts for a moment.] depressed. And... [Satanic timpanic drumroll.] you are *still* in Hell!
Justin:	[Shrugs.] If I'm being honest, I stopped trying to figure out my whereabouts with all of the hands, doors, and gates appearing. I figured somebody would tell me eventually. May I leave?
Freud:	You may not! You are still depressed.
Justin:	You've had me in a straightjacket for quite a long time. Depression is bound to happen.
Freud:	It's called therapy my depressed tragedian.
Justin:	I'm not a doctor or specialist on the matter but isn't therapy supposed to heal or at least remedy?
Freud:	You are correct; you are not a doctor. So if you don't mind, shut up, and get better.
Polaris:	I'm starting to feel better, good doctor. [Shines to prove it.] May I leave?
Freud:	No! [*Polaris* dims, *Room* squeals, and an imagined chandelier of blood shatters, spilling garnet and crystal onto a pooled Persian rug. *Room* is terrified.]
Room:	I don't want to be here! [Looks for an exit. Sees none.]
Chair 2:	Everyone, calm down. [Hands *Room* a handkerchief. To *Justin*.] So how are you feeling since we last spoke?

Justin:	I'm not sure. I'm still here, so I guess that means I haven't progressed.
Chair 2:	[Checks the notes.] That's awfully interesting. Did we talk about your relationship with your family?
Justin:	No, and I don't care to. When I last spoke with the good doctor, [*Freud* is busy again asleep while interpreting the dreamscape. *Polaris* shines over him as an over-bloomed moon.] we were discussing trauma and trying to describe my aesthetic.
Chair 2:	Yes, I'm well aware; I was there. So would you mind telling me a little bit about your family?
Carpe Diem:	I wasn't though! It's not every day we get a writer in Hell. [For a moment, *Dante, Milton*, and all the great writers who spoke of Hell, shatter.] How did you describe your aesthetic?
Freud:	[Wakes up briefly.] Watered-down surrealism! [Resumes his unconscious study. He dreams of *Room* undressing her silked voice, hello good doctor, bed sheets waiting to be drawn away, ruffling in anticipation, hello good doctor, how the light laces around the interplay of their shadows, oh god, hands his, belonging to, my good doctor, sleek and slip against *Room's* padded walls, against the room, against the door, against the carry of her excess flesh sensuously, the padded walls to water and flower, hello good doctor, velvet the cheek too pressed, suede sung unshaven against it, the meaning growing into interpretation, padded walls panting to keep him laced and ivory, the inkblots of their bodies where they begin and end, no, the door as the exit of seduction, locked and knobbed, hello my good doctor, whisper it again for the fantasized keepsake, but that voice, and how he wants to be the hollow sound inside it, hello good doctor, hello good doctor, calves each time to tremble, bedpost the treble clef to octave, *Room's* fingers roped against his throat, tighter the whisper, the tongue constellating against his most intimate fears, unlocked, unresolved, unstudied, hello good doctor, the until, the bleed of blue, the mind night-chambered locked wandering inside, writhing in aimless euphoria, the destination backwards, what

it all means, meaning, thusly, and then after.]

Justin: [Shrugs. To *Chair 2*.] I don't really want to talk about it.

Chair 2: [Checks the notes.] It says here that talking about trauma is therapeutic.

Justin: The point being to gain perspective, correct?

Chair 2: [Checks the notes, while twirling an imagined finely tuned mustache.] Correct.

[*Justin* is quiet. Silence ensues.]

[*Freud* wakes up, soiled in a sticky mess, his head resting against *Room's* padded opoponax; the scented chest. *Freud* reclines stiffly on *Couch* and interprets his unconscious notes; *how do I describe my scent when I'm lost in the taste of yours?* Odd.]

Freud: [After readjusting his stained dress shirt and crookedly cracked glasses.] Well my mentally unstable charges, I have another appointment to catch! [He looks up, his right hand points to the padded ceiling, he clicks his heels together. Descends!]

[*Freud* descends through the roof below, where *Oedipus* is reading.]

Oedipus: [Caught in the netting of *Bloodletting*.] Hello again, good doctor. I take it you're familiar with this? [Shows the book to *Freud*.]

Freud: Unfortunately.

Oedipus: Well, what do you make of it?

Freud: [Swats at an imagined buzzing sound.] Exactly.

Oedipus: I see. [Returns to the pages.]

Freud: [Continues.] It's what I've been trying to tell people for years.

Oedipus:	[Looks up.] Tell us what?
Freud:	Mothers!
Oedipus:	What's wrong with you?
Freud:	[The buzzing grows to a voice calling for 3 measures of gin, 1 measure of vodka, a vermouthed pinch of brined tuna, and a messy splash of wrist-opening. Stir with a finger. Limb and body my voice to garnish. Citrus and then drink.] Pardon?
Oedipus:	What do you mean? I understand that there's attachment here, but that doesn't necessarily mean anything sexual or inappropriate. It's intimate, surely, but sexual? Is there a physical desire there?
Freud:	[Grabs the book from *Oedipus*. Shakes the unripened pages free.] Did you get to the chair scene?
Oedipus:	Yes, but if anything—
Freud:	[The voice is screaming its thirst! *Freud* grabs *Oedipus*, too close, spraying his words laced with sour spit.] Did you understand the repetition? *Was there a purpose in your mother's suffering, was there a purpose in your mother's suffering, was there a purpose in your mother's suffering?*
Oedipus:	You mean the conclusion?
Freud:	The climax!
Oedipus:	What's wrong with you?
Freud:	And his insistence on blood, did you understand?
Oedipus:	I think people in your field call this 'warped tunnel vision complex,' or scorched interpretation universe syndrome.
Freud:	Q: And what does the 'tunnel' represent? A: The uterus.

Oedipus: [Looks at *Bloodletting* differently now.] You're right! What's wrong with me?

Freud: [He lets go and faux-academically adjusts his glasses.] You married your mother, and your children are your forefathers.

Oedipus: How did this happen?

Freud: Well, for starters, you have a drinking problem.

Oedipus: [Takes a syringe filled with mercurial Ambrosia.] I believe you.

Freud: And I'm here. That's usually a bad sign. I tend to read into things. I usually bring up thoughts that should rather be left untouched.

Oedipus: I love her though. What's wrong with me?

Freud: People are strange. Think about it. We created a system of divine imperfect beings with personality problems, neuroses, sexual impotency, infidelity divinations, children like yours, born from the wrong anatomical parts, killing fathers, mothers unhappy. [Begins doodling *Chaos* in a vulnerable pose, and crumbles it after a few strokes.]

Oedipus: Is that why we're all here in this place?

Freud: You mean Hell? That's what we call it now, you know.

Oedipus: I don't like it. It reminds me of my father. [The room is shaped to *Oedipus'* father, somehow sharing a likeness to *The Can*.]

Freud: [Falls asleep, at ease in this room, letting the ensuing dream remain unstudied.] Yes, and I cannot help you.

[Back to *Chair 2, Justin, Polaris, Carpe Diem*, and an undressed *Room*.]

Chair 2:   [To *Justin*.] You have yet to say anything of significance.

Polaris: I'm bored! I'm bored! [*Polaris* floats up to play the role of *The Sun* in the room's night-sky.]

Justin: My brother is an addict, so of course our relationship isn't great.

Chair 2:   Nonsense! I know many addicts who are close to their brothers.
              Plus, who are you to cast the first stone, if you catch my drift.

Justin: My brother is dying.

Chair 2:   Oh, I'm sure you are just being a little theatrical.

Justin: My brother is an addict, dying.

Chair 2:   You really enjoy repetition.

Justin: [Grabs *Room*, *Polaris*, *Carpe Diem* slouched in the corner,
              the light, the sounds, the whimper, *The Chairs*, the setting, the
              scale that tips, the dialogue, the silence that would vacuum
              after, all to something fire and sharp.] My brother is fucking
              dying and because of his addiction he is doing it to himself,
              dying, and how it affects the mother with the womb, and
              the father as the shepherd, [Tears at the walls, the room, and
              everything.] so I leave and tear at walls, but you can't just
              distance yourself, and you just want to shake his shoulders,
              bear words that will move him away from addiction, and it is
              unimaginably, infinitesimally, abysmally frustrating for others
              to say he is an addict like he is helpless against it, the song
              against the muting wind and bleeding wave, and each needled
              pinch to his skin a decision he made, and really, I believe he is
              not good, or noble, and to commit his addiction to art would
              be against everything that I've crafted, and I was going to be a
              fucking uncle, meaning he was going to be a father, twice now,
              but each one lost, each child lost, he is an addict, an addict, like
              that's supposed to fucking validate what he did, because it's an
              illness, and I am his brother, Justin, my name is Justin, and my
              brother is an addict, and he has an illness, and he has stolen,
              cheated, pawned, lied, beaten, threatened at gunpoint, cried,
              apologized, pawned, lied, and beaten, each time returning
              to his addictions, escalating each time, cocaine, bath salts,
              methamphetamine, pills, OxyContin, heroin, and it breaks,

it breaks, it fucking breaks, and brings the ugliness out of the people I love, and they become fragile and trembled, because they can't distance themselves like I have, as I lie to you, and say that I've distanced myself from him, see? See?! Do you fucking see me lying to you? I don't care! I don't care! I don't care! But he should have died at this point, overdosing on it three times already, his heart should have stopped, the same heart, kissed, touched, and tasted by the needle's piercing caress, the one that took away my brother, *No! ceci n'est pas une seringue, ceci n'est pas un frère d'armes de violet, no, indigo. No! Bleu renversé! Ma mère, à cause de lui* because because because of him…

[The dance ends. The room-sky is broken, *Room* just padded walls again, quiet the beating blows, *Polaris* as a cracked sun on the floor whimpering. *Justin*, with fists still raining down on the fallen star, finally drops, unbuttoned as a character. The door closes, *Justin* lost in a memory.]

I remember I was in bed, in the top bunk.
I remember telling him to turn the lights off.
We argued briefly. I didn't want to climb down my little red ladder.
I don't even remember being tired.

I remember telling him to turn the lights off. He finally said yes,
climbed out from his sheets, flicked the switch, room now dark as an
unadjusting image, the red ladder I didn't climb down, no, I wasn't tired,
and as he came back with his little steps, hear the pitched clink as he trips.

The room goes dark, as the light switch flicks, fine I'll do it.
I remember the door being flung open, your hair disheveled and bleached
blonde [Enter *Mom.*], you didn't hear the clink as he tripped, but his
scream. As you rush in, the room a sharp note of light again, reveals the
blood.

With your hair disheveled and bleached, you grabbed me, screaming *god damnit Justin*, the descending half step from light to dark, we were so young back then, the light notes of blood shaded sounds from his lip, your younger response to it, the bearer of it later. I remember how you gripped my hair.

My descending scene of half steps where I am supposed to turn the light off, where my brother is bleeding because I didn't, the anti-bearer of light, as I wriggle and squirm away from you pulling my hair, yelling, I remember it, too young for this tempo, running to the bathroom, now tired, door locked.

My brother is bleeding, as I try to get away from you with my little steps, trying to grasp the loose threads of a violent comprehension, hiding in the bathroom. Yes, I was tired now.
Why were you so angry with me? Why did you need to hit me? Remember.

In that bathroom, grasping the frayed threading of a tired comprehension, I've never been more afraid of you and I remember realizing that maybe I didn't get my temper from just my father. You didn't need to hit me; I was already sorry. [Enter a blinding quiet, as I unlock the bathroom door.]

I have never been more afraid of you in the dark, as my unbuttoned steps led me back to the room. I closed the bedroom door behind me tender softly, and already sorry, climbed the little red ladder to my bed. The room closes its eyes; a quiet blinding sets in with the soured wet left behind after tasteless.

A tight grip, dry mouth, numb warmth circled around the eyes.
You had him with you, embraced and quietly hurting with a chipped tooth.
I remember the dark, unsettled tide of the room; a dark light caressed to a swelling silence. Here I close my eyes (eigengrau), growing smaller in sleep.

Confrontation Movement 2

[*Freud* knocks on the door, and enters with *Bloodletting*, limbed with arms and legs, gnawing on the bone of a charred chair leg. *Freud* directs *Bloodletting*, who crawls on its haunches, to lead *Justin* over to *Stage*, where a sober *Jason*, his *Mother*, and *An Unspoken Poem* greet him in silence.]

Justin: [Now wearing a fake beard to illustrate over-dramatically that quite a bit of time has passed. He shields his eyes, even though the stage is only dimly lit.] How long have I been in that room?

Freud: [Checks his pocket watch and laughs.] I could tell you, but it doesn't really matter. How do you feel?

Justin: I—

Freud: Oh Jesus, forget I asked! It's time for this scene to begin, and you're too busy sputtering your self-pitying nonsense words. Anyway, this scene is supposed to begin any second now, and you are already familiar with my stance on punctuality I hope. And with that said, [Checks the pocket watch again.] that's it for me. I'll be taking my leave.

Justin: No, you mustn't!

Freud: Oh, but I must! You see, I have no more lines left!

[*Freud* leaves and takes his seat in *The Audience* on *Chair 2*.]

Exit *Freud*.

Jason: [After a silent while, points at *Bloodletting*, still gnawing on the bone.] What is that?

Justin: [To *Jason* and *Mom*.] I wrote you a body.

[*Bloodletting*, ears perked, begins mumbling a low key.]

Mom: [Looking away from their resemblance; *Jason*, *Mom*, and *Justin*.] What is it saying?

Justin: How should I know?

[*Bloodletting* mumbles louder now, but still inaudible; a dirge assertion.]

Jason: [Almost dreaming.] It smells.

Mom: [To *Justin*.] You did this?

Justin: [Goes over to *Mom* and gently switches wrists, his now
                  becoming slender and pale tapering. *Justin* slits it, reopening
                  the scarred line, feeding his work.]

[*Bloodletting* becomes more articulate.]

Bloodletting: [The low dirge forming, shaking the walls, the pillars, the
                  ground above now crashing down dramatically.] There are
                  words inside me, there are words inside me, there are words
                  inside me... [Repeat each time with a different meaning,
                  the first and last pages flapping in a cleavered open portrait
                  embrace, all the music inside lost above them, untethered,
                  crying out all at once, a concerto for all ill-fitting parts in all
                  scales, all at once, shouting and whispering what I couldn't
                  say, how feelings change over time, how we revert back to not
                  knowing what to say to each other. *Justin* sets *Bloodletting* in a
                  fed fetal position. *Bloodletting* claws all characters away, climbs
                  up the wall, arms, torso, and shape phantom. *Bloodletting* spits
                  out *Light*, blinds all to *Sight*. A scene is flickering in front of
                  Jason's family. Something with hooves and horns holds *Jason's*
                  head pointed facing the scene. He cannot escape.]

Justin: [To *Jason* speaking speechless.] I'm not ready for this yet.

Bloodletting: This has to end.

Jason: This isn't my fault!

Justin: [Turns knifed towards his brother. He sees his brother relenting
                  for the first time.] You know that it is though. I think that's
                  why you split into something dark, and sad that night.

Jason: I don't.

Justin: You do, though. I think that's why you're lost.

[*Justin* looks away from his brother, and sees *Mom* cradled in the arms of all *Justin's* forgotten characters in an embrace, without *Justin's* direction; there is empathy and warmth here in this moment. *Justin* is blank with too many thoughts and expressions. All the characters face what *Bloodletting* projects.]

[Scene: The kitchen. The anger that carries over the voices.

Mom is yelling through a door. *Mom* found that there are parts missing in *Jason's* story. *Jason* has been leaving the house at 3:00 am. The doors were locked, alarms set, the windows closed. *Jason* has not been acting correctly. We all want him better. We don't want to see him leave again. We want him to want this with us. So the door is locked, windows closed, and the alarms set tight. But *Jason* leaves us, appearing at 3:00 am, inside someone who isn't supposed to be there. *Jason* has been coming home high with her smirking behind him. This is his first time back home from prison. He was gone at a point where he didn't feel present. He had a gun, and there was cocaine inside him like a cloud, I don't know why this happens, and there will be a scene where we are told his heart should have failed, stopping him. But here he is, home now and sneaking a girl into the house at 3:00 am, supplying him with pills and poetry. *Mom* is yelling at *Jason* through the door. *Mom* threatens to call the police. The girl is yelling at *Mom* through the door. *Jason* is yelling at *Mom* through the door. The door listens to both sides, remaining locked and objective. The girl relents, and disappears. *Jason* storms out, stumbling straight, yelling at *Mom*. *Mom* tells *Jason* she thinks he is selling his ADHD medication, remembering that first it was cocaine. She sees him as a repetitive action. *Jason* calls her words leading up to a 'cunt' finale. *Jason* disappears, leaving his words behind to phantom. *Dad* tries to remain objective, like the door. *Mom* hasn't been acting like herself since *Jason* appeared again, disappeared again. *Dad* has been getting worse since. *Mom* is yelling at *Dad*. *Dad* opens and responds, 'It's your fault he is like this.' *Mom* runs to the kitchen. There is a cleaver within reach. The cleaver sinks across her wrist. The doctor tells her to cut vertically next time.]

[It's important that this is repeated, the only way I'll feel better. *Like a pantoum?* Yes.] Did you know mom tried to kill herself? [*Justin* grabs *Bloodletting*, points the light hard and violent into *Jason's* corneas, blurred into focus. Closer and closer, until the images condense, breathing heavily onto his face, in and out like something hungry to chew on. *Justin* won't let *Bloodletting* go, the light sputtering on.]

Jason: [Shriveled and sinking in.] Did you know mom tried to kill herself?

Dad: [Did you know—]

Justin: [To *Dad*, interrupting the stage direction.] Mom said your words led her across her wrist.

Dad: [{Sinking across}—your mother tried to kill herself? {the lone bright star fades to ink}.]

[The forgotten planted mask of *Romulus* sprouts, forming a perfect copy of *Justin* {a rose shatters off-stage}. The reflection takes his seat with the others, staring blankly at *Bloodletting* dripping image and memory on *Jason*.]

Justin: [To his copy.] Did you know mom tried to kill herself?

[A dud goes off. *Justin*, as both person and reflection, shatters. A rose blooms on-stage. *All of Hell's Moons* fall from their chandeliered stars. *Time*, bleeding out in an inked tub, flickers out.]

Jason: [Maybe seeing for the first time his brother ruined in a dead language because of his actions.] I'm awake now.

[*Justin* looks up.]

I'm [Opening.] here.

Chair 3:   Where are you now?

Jason: With my actions, and the people who hold me with them.

Chair 3:   How would you best describe yourself?

[*Justin* snaps his fingers, hoping. *Bloodletting* snaps, flickers off to *Fin*.]

Jason: I'm [Shaking.] my mother's slender, my father's shade.

[*Justin*, knees folded on the face of a fallen moon, praying in this place.]

Chair 3:   Do you know what you've done?

[*Jason* is in the final throes of convulsion, the question unchambered from the barrel, words resonant for once, *Justin* with those eyes, with that fucking look!, pictured memory melodied, yes, maybe I didn't need to, but he… the choir phantoms to escape as *Justin* approaches wearing the outcome of their last fight, nose broken, an eye swollen shut, lip split and still bleeding. He hands his brother the notebook given to him by *Freud*. *Jason* opens up the notebook (mostly torn pages and teeth marks), and finds a remaining line: *Brother, even now, if you called for purple, I would give you amethyst from my mouth; if blue, water and a sail.*]

[Quietly, a firm hand softly on the shoulder.] Do you know what you've done?

Jason: I am [Please say it this time.]/

[Chthonic white space
reflecting {remembers}
Chthonic white space.]

…guilty.

[*Justin* goes to him and places a wreath of amethyst and ocean over him. *Justin* then steps back, and becomes the background.]

Dad: [*Jason* dips a finger into a pearl-rusted pool, reaches for his father, and draws a forgiving symbol on his forehead. *Dad* sees their shared depth and embraces him.] I am guilty too.

Mom: [Looking at the bodies of *The Fallen Moons* and to all
                 characters gathered. She traces the line on her wrist.] I am
                 sorry.

                 [*Justin* lands softly, and kisses his mother. He becomes a quiet song.]

Jason: [Goes to his mother, his hands filled with warmth, delicately
                 ripple against her cheek.] I am {with the expression of a fallen
                 moon looking up at the empty night canvas} sorry.

                 [*Justin* lanterns *All of Hell* with a birdcage holding the fluttering *Sun*.
                 The End and *All*, an embraced bow, disappearing.]

Epilogue

[All characters head to the front of *Stage* to greet *Audience*.]

Freud: [Standing ovation from his seat.] Magnifique! Truly! Mah-Nih-Phi-Que! Bravo all! I had such a wonderful nap! Merci! [Throws to *Stage* a bouquet of Freudian dreams sleeping like an articulate nightmare.]

Chair 2: [To *Freud*.] Liar! I saw you taking notes.

Freud: [Raises his hands in innocence.] Yes, yes, guilty your High Chair. I was joking. [Checks his notes.] I thought it was very good. May I go back to sleep now? I have much more important work to finish.

Justin: Did you really think it was good?

Freud: Too bad I couldn't cure that lyrical insecurity of yours.

Justin: Well, what did you at least think of the ending?

Freud: Let's ask them. [Directs everyone's attention theatrically to three cloaked figures in the audience.] Lights please! And if you would be so kind as to reveal yourselves for dramatic effect, I would be ever so grateful.

[The characters lower their hoods to reveal *Mom*, *Dad*, and a sleeping *Jason*. *Mom* is emotional, *Dad* is quiet, and *Jason* is caught in a suspiciously deep sleep. The staged *Dad*, *Mom*, and *Jason* step forward, and uproot their masks revealing; *Zeus*, *Ceres*, and *Bacchus*. *Justin* seeing the masks rootless, grows silent, quietly shaking. *Freud* notes *Justin's* shaking.]

Zeus: [To *Justin*.] Well? How did we do?

[*Justin* continues to silently shake. *Zeus* continues to speak, seeking assurances from unconscious ears not awake to meaning anymore. Seeing assurances as an impossible task with *Justin* in the throes of daze, *Bacchus* begins to dance and chant a *Dionysian* song, slits his wrist with a night-labyrinth's fang, an ocean of vintaged wine flooding out. *Stage* drinks hungrily. *Zeus* takes a long drink too, and turns into a silk-folded swan. *Ceres* chariots onto him, lips pressed against flight, melody, and wine, the opaline glow of a warm winter garden. *Freud* sees this scene of chaotic feathered streaks against nape and navel, and his hand subconsciously slips—]

Chair 2:   [To *Freud*.] You're disgusting.

Freud: What do you mean? It's beautiful!

Chair 2:   But aren't Ceres and Zeus…

Freud: [Shrugs.] Who am I to judge? I'm just a therapist.

Chair 2:   I'm just a chair, but I still find it pretty gross.

[*Freud* ignores *Chair 2* and continues. *Chair 2* throws a dream manifesto at *Freud*.]

        Seriously, stop. [Points to *Justin*. *Justin* is now mumbling inaudibly.] We have to help him. This won't end until we do.

Freud: Fine. [To *Justin*.] Speak up! The good audience can't hear you!

Justin: I was saying that the last scene should be the ending.

Freud: Incorrect. It was a nice scene, but a terrible ending.

Justin: Why?

Freud: Because it wasn't an honest conclusion.

Justin: What do you mean? Of course it was honest. I expressed how I really feel.

Freud: Yes, you shared your feelings to actors who read their lines very well.

[*Justin* is quiet for a while. *Freud* tiptoes his gaze back towards the chants and moans of the wine pantheon scene. *Chair 2* gives him a sharp chair-legged blow to the ribs.]

Justin: I didn't know they were actors.

Freud: And whose fault is that?

Justin: But it felt so...

Freud: Ideal. You wrote an *ideal* ending.

Justin: That isn't how things normally end, is it?

Freud: No, which is why I have deduced that you are depressed.

Justin: Yes, I believe you are right, good doctor.

Freud: It is quite sad, really, you have my condolences. But I want this to end honestly. So, I ask again the all-important question; was there a purpose to everyone's suffering?

Justin: [Looks deeply into the real *Mom*, *Dad*, and *Jason* in the audience. He sees his brother shaking, looking too thin and worn, suspiciously frail, drawn close to an end and needle marked. *Justin's* mouth moves wordless, eclipsed with the infinite measures of breath between yes and no. All of his characters gather before him; created from trauma, his expression of it.] I...

[*Freud* snaps a quill, which becomes
a broken mirror. *Freud* drags it
towards *Justin*. *Justin's* reflection
twists and turns, blooms into focus,
an exact replication,
Justin inebriated on the sounds
of trauma, the ending
suffering its beginnings,
the grip of it loosening to a constricting
caress, my brother as the loved disease.

Justin's reflection as an out of focus bloom,
more realistic that way, inebriated
in artless applause of the last scene.
The last scene inarticulate in an ideal
conclusion, but needed to be written that way
because I love them with a constricting caress,
while the broken mirror looks
for my diseased brother, to reflect
how outside of this staged direction, he remains
repetitive, reshaping his ending
and how everyone I care about descends
further into red each time.

The scene where my brother admits his guilt
is an ideal conclusion, inarticulate but needed,
because the truth is, he will die
and I know that beneath these words, there is a dirge
repeating that I can't reshape
how I love him, despite how I blame him
for so much, how his ending is self-
inflicted, how my mother breaks and father drinks,
how I do both a little quieter,
while whispering to you in verse.

Because the truth is, I will lose you, my
brother, beneath these words,
an act of burial as you still live,
hoping you will read this before then
and know that I remember everything
we both did and lost to each other,

and yes, I know she broke spilling
on the floor, and dad,
hear it in his voice, hear it
in his voice, drinks,
because the truth is, we lose ourselves
each time for choosing you
over an ideal ending.

I hope you will read these words
and remember
that there was a time when you were drowning,
not as metaphor, but 6 or 7 years old,
in the deep end of the pool, and you couldn't swim,
screaming all the theatrics of drowning,
and I dove in after you, carried you up to surface.
Remember when I visited you in prison
each time, each time you were there
when I said I didn't want to, because I didn't
want to, but still, imagine the saddest road trip
that goes on for hours, four hours each way, repeated
again and again,
because you were so far away, because the truth
is, I lost the meaning to it, the repeated question,
because what meaning is there when you are
dying a self-inflicted death, feeling helpless with
the words, when the ending we all want is idealized,
but makes more sense, is more rational than the present.

I said I didn't want to after getting the first phone call,
and you need to know that dad came after me,

[Hear it in his voice.]

the sentences we exchanged, broken currents of syntax

grabbing and pulling incoherently and timpani

into each other, an octave rising

then submerged by a louder voice

with an angry film glazed over the eyes, (remember

the numbing sound as he swung,

the smell of red connecting)

because, I didn't want to

because, I didn't fucking want to.

But I ended up driving mom to see you

at the police station, the first time it happened,

and I had to be the one to identify you

even though you were

the unfamiliar shape, with the wisps of white hair,

slender and shouldered,

shouting in tongue your improvised French

je parle faux francaise,

remember the sound of mom pleading for you to be good,

as we learned that you hit someone with a pistol,

he almost lost his eye, did you know that?

learned how far you were gone from us,

the meaning of incoherent explained

with each word you shattered,

and how this happened again, incoherent

with solutions, and again,

incoherent and quiet.

Brother, your ending will be self-inflicted,

because it keeps happening, escalating to an end,

but let these words of me

loving you be repeated

of me loving you, and know that if

it weren't for you, my words wouldn't be

so vibrant in tragedy, rendering my art worthless.

So what I am now, no, what we all are now,

shaped by you, not knowing the value

of it, as the question gets repeated.

Was there a purpose in your mother's suffering?

Was there a purpose in your father's suffering?

What is the purpose of my suffering?

My brother will die, and

my mother tried to, and I will write after this

that the *Audience* applauds, calls for

an encore after the curtain falls,

throwing bouquets of ancient flowers

and exotic birds, and tearing at their eyes

and hair, storming the stage with applause

for more! for more! for more!

all while I blur into the impossible figure

of your brother broken with the weight

of the repeated words of loving you.

> [*Justin* opens the lanterned birdcage that blankets *Stage* with *Light,*
> releasing *The Sun* inside. He plants it inside the chest of a now quiet
> and unmoving *Stage.* After pouring a strange song of water, *The Sun*
> blooms into a fluttering *Snow Moon. Justin* plucks it still-tender and
> places it on his word-burial for his brother; all characters watching.
> *Mom* reaches him and places her hand which has whispered red before
> on his shoulder. Hell's horizon sets.]

Justin Limoli is a writer and horticulturist.
He lives in New York, NY.

I would like to take this opportunity to thank *On Romulus*. So many times, I almost gave up on you. And yet, you lingered. You took all the time and patience I didn't think I had. And now you exist and I love you.

And on that note, thank you *Bloodletting*. Did you know you were going to be a character in your sequel? Could you even guess there would even be a sequel? Truthfully, I didn't until that sad warmth of your last line started to fade and there seemed to be a piece missing. You are my poetry. *On Romulus* is my play. Let no one say that you are not the more beautiful.

Thank you to my publisher/editing genius, Tyler Crumrine. Thank you for your patience, as I filled your inbox with incessant edits. You will never know just how much I needed your guidance on this.

Thank you, Maui. You were a beautiful and complicated little island far away in the Pacific. I miss you, my flowers, and everything that bloomed there

To all the writers/playwrights in Plays Inverse; it is amazing to see how I'm not the only one who thought this form is a good idea. And more importantly, thank you for demonstrating that this form works on the stage just as well as on the page. I am in great company.

Thank you *Justin* (the character… and me a little bit, too). Thank you for reaching the end without breaking, and articulating lines I needed to hear. I think we are going to be okay.

And finally, thank you dear reader. Without you, this would go unread. I sincerely hope you were moved.